MY JOURNEY ON THE ROAD TO EMMAUS

Memoirs of a Pastor's wife

Diana E. Linn

Diana Linn's Publishing LLC
6398 S. Wheaton Dr
Tucson Arizona

Any future Pastor or Pastor's Wife contemplating or praying for God's guidance, wisdom and direction should read **My Journey on the Road to Emmaus, Memoirs of a Pastor's Wife**, if they are interested in Christian Ministry.

Diana would be the first to acknowledge the less mistakes made in your young ministry, the more glory to God. The Linn's together have a total of over fifty years in Alliance ministry. But greater than that is the firsthand experience gleamed through all these years of ministry together.

You may laugh, cry or you might even shake your head with the thought *I'd better pray more to make sure this is what God really wants for me.* That's right ladies, it was and still is quite an adventure being a Pastor's wife.

ON THE ROAD TO EMMAUS (Luke 24 NLT)

Walking along On the Road to Emmaus ... saddened by the crucifixion, two of Jesus disciples began discussing all that had happened. They had believed that Jesus was the Messiah, but now he has been crucified.

As they walked along, they were talking about everything that had happened. ... Jesus himself suddenly came and began walking with them. But God kept them from recognizing him.

... Jesus said to them, "You, foolish people! You find it so hard to believe all that the prophets wrote in the Scriptures. Wasn't it clearly predicted that the Messiah would have to suffer all these things before entering his glory?" Then Jesus took them through the writings of Moses and all the prophets, explaining from all the Scriptures the things concerning himself.

As they neared "Emmaus and the end of their journey, Jesus acted as if he were going on, but they begged him, "Stay the night with us, since it is getting late." So, he went home with them. As they sat down to eat, he took the bread and blessed it. Then he broke it and gave it to them. **Suddenly, their eyes were opened, and they recognized him.** And at that moment he disappeared!

Shortly after this occurrence, Jesus came and told his disciples, "I have been given all authority in heaven and on earth. Therefore, go and make disciples of all the nations, baptizing them in the name of the Father and the Son and the Holy Spirit. Teach these new disciples to obey all the commands I have given you. And be sure of this: I am with you always, even to the end of the age" (**Matthew 28:19-20**)

My Journey on The Road to Emmaus is that I would be willing to share the Jesus of the New Testament. So, we can be instrumental in bringing back the King as our Savior. May that be my testimony throughout this book.

Copyright © 2019 Diana E. Linn

All rights reserved. No part of this publication may be reproduced, distributed, or transmitted in any form or by any means, including photocopying, recording, or other electronic or mechanical methods, without the prior written permission of the publisher, except in the case of brief quotations embodied in critical reviews and certain other noncommercial uses permitted by copyright law. **For permission requests**, write to the publisher, at the address below.

The events portrayed in *My Journey on the Road to Emmaus, Memoirs of a Pastor's Wife* is the author's recollection of events, and that some identities may have been changed or are composites of characters only. Some characters and events in this book may be fictitious only to tell a story of facts and any similarity to real persons, living or dead, in those cases are coincidental and not intended by the author.

Editing by Editor Robert T. Linn/Diana E. Linn/Author

Front cover image by Robert T. Linn/B & D Photography

All photographs by Diana E. Linn/Robert T. Linn unless otherwise credited

Diana Linn's Publishing, LLC, 6398 S. Wheaton Dr., Tucson AZ 85747; **Ordering Information**: Contact the publisher at the address above. Copies may be purchased via e-mail: bdlinn@icloud.com or Amazon.com as well as BarnesandNoble.com

Printed in the United States of America

Category of the Book: Biography.

ISBN 978-0-9980819-0-8

First Edition

DEDICATION

This book is especially dedicated to my husband, Bert Linn. During the months it took me to write my memoirs around the excitement of our ministry together has been a tremendous blessing. God has used us in His Service for Kingdom Glory and we are ever grateful to be able to relate how God has led the both of us and to share this journey with our readers. My husband was my encourager as I passionately wrote on hopefully for God's Glory.

INTRODUCTION

This is the humorous side of the pastoral ministry from the view point of a minister's wife.

In the writing of this book I found it to be gratifying in seeing how God led in the many ways that so often we wouldn't have chosen except for God's very obvious leading. It never was a mystery to us, God always *made the way straight* so that we could see *this is the way, walk in it*, it is *my plan*.

To begin my story, I felt it important to reach into the early beginnings of my family and how it all led to God's calling for me. How He was going to lead instead of me finding my own way. From the time I came to know my Savior, there has never been an occasion where I would have preferred another way outside of God's plan. How does anyone get through life without God?

In the ministerial life for both my husband and I, we always knew full well when God was calling and to where He was calling. Circumstances aren't always easy, especially when dealing with people but God knows that. Nothing escapes Him, He knows where we are to go next even if it is to wait on Him for a time. He also put us in predicaments so that when we wanted to *give it up*, logically we just couldn't. So, you tie a knot at the end of your rope and hang on. The answer is on the way.

My attempt in this book is to show when we are in the heat of the battle there still is a humorous side of the ministry. Remember, though we are in combat with Satan, and though he always wants to stop us from reaching people for Christ, God has already won that battle. After all, it is His will for all of us to be Great Commission Christians.

Each church ministry had its bloopers, as we journeyed in our walk with the Lord, but Jesus has everything covered with his blood. He died so that we could live. We only have to accept that. He already paid our debt for yesterday, today and forever. We simply have to say, forgive me Jesus. The worry is gone. He gives us beauty for ashes and then lights the fire in our soul so that we can fulfill the Great Commission together and He will go with us to the very end. Enjoy!

CONTENTS

MY JOURNEY ON THE ROAD TO EMMAUS
(Luke 24 NLT)
Memoirs of a Pastor's wife

Diana E. Linn

On the Road to Emmaus (Luke 24 NLT) i
Copyright © 2019 Diana E. Linn ii
Dedication iii
Introduction iv
Chapter ONE
    Ancestral Origins 1
Chapter TWO
    My Families Beginning 9
Chapter THREE
    The Great Depression 13
Chapter FOUR
    Sometimes It Hurts 17
Chapter FIVE
    Illness In Turmoil 27
Chapter SIX
    The Invitation 29
Chapter SEVEN
    The Move 33
Chapter EIGHT
    The Call 41
Chapter NINE
    Walking the Call 45
Chapter TEN
    The Preparation 65
Chapter ELEVEN
    Meeting My Husband 85

Chapter TWELVE
　　Joyce Bible Church
　　Our First Church Together 89
Chapter THIRTEEN
　　So, Send I You
　　Shelton Alliance Church 115
Chapter FOURTEEN
　　Roseburg Alliance Church 125
Chapter FIFTEEN
　　Following the Call 129
Chapter SIXTEEN
　　The Long Beach Rescue Mission 135
Chapter SEVENTEEN
　　Hope Alliance Church
　　　　An Inner-City Mission Church 141
Chapter EIGHTEEN
　　CrossPoint Community Church
　　A Church of the Christian & Missionary Alliance 149
Chapter NINETEEN
　　Alliance Bible Church 157
Chapter TWENTY
　　The Road Church 161
Chapter TWENTY-ONE
　　Epilogue
　　"But the End is Not Yet" (Mark 137) 163
Testimony for Bert & Diana Linn 168
One Last Thing 167
Biographical History 171
END NOTES 174

My Journey on the Road to Emmaus   Diana E. Linn

Chapter ONE
Ancestral Origins

Surely, it would have been a cold snowy day in February, the ground cold and crisp with snow still lightly falling. Normal for Ukraine, (in the early part of the 19th Century, was then a part of Russia). It would be on a day like this that my Grandmother would go into labor and give birth. Mother was born in my Grandparent's home, in the early 1900s. In those days, there would only be Mid-wives to assist in the birth unless by chance the doctor was in the area caring for others at the same time.

Winter was never an easy time. It wouldn't be long before Grandfather would move the entire family to their beautiful home in Siberia where temperatures often fell to 88 degrees below zero with summers reaching balmy 65 degrees.

"We're going to be moving girls. You will have to pack everything together so that we can load the buggy."

"Why? Lena wanted to know.

"It's to a much larger home. It will be more comfortable for all of us. You know that I have to be away most of the time and I want to know you are safe. It gets worrisome living here when I can't be near you."

"Remember girls, your Father has a lot of men to lead in the Military. That's a very demanding job."

Years later Mother tried describing to me all the splendor of the home, in its architectural beauty. Not only that but the artistic design and decor that filled the home. The family wanted for nothing.

Mother and her family would live in Siberia into her teenage years when she and her Father would make an attempt to escape the Communism take-over with only the clothes on their backs 1918-19 to emigrate into Canada.

"If we can't take anything, how will we survive, Father?"

"God will take care of us." In confidence, he would repeat over and over, "God will take care of us."

Mother told us endless stories and horrific incidents on their plight to arrive in St. Petersburg awaiting passage from their sponsor, the Mennonite Central Relief Committee, to emigrate into Canada.

They boarded the ship and as the days continued on, Mother says she became extremely ill.

"I'm going to die, Father."

"You are not going to die on this Ship. You are only seasick."

Upon arriving on the east coast of Canada, they were located in the City of Winnipeg, Manitoba where families would hire the Russian immigrants, often as housemaids, cooks and the like. It was no wonder a city like Winnipeg was experiencing a dramatic growth by the late 19th and early 20th centuries. It was there that Ana, my mother worked off the expense of transport for her father, sister and herself. Though my mother's sister's passage was paid, she was never able to leave Russia. I'm told her passage was forfeited and given to someone else and upon that discovery, shortly thereafter she died.

Then on my Father's side, my Grandfather, Johann Penner, and Maria Classen fell in love while living in Landon-Cavalier, North Dakota.

Let me paint the scene.

There they were, all alone walking in the meadow. Talking and making plans that they imagined could be theirs.

"What do you want us to do, Johann, in our future? How many children should we have?"

"Of course, we'll have children, they are a blessing from God. But, Maria, I want us to do more."

"What more can we do? We can have a farm, just like your family has always done."

"I'd like to raise cattle and maybe I could even become a blacksmith."

"Maybe. Isn't it fun to dream of our future?"

To them, it seemed like love had captured them. Why not?

"Oh, Johann."

"Marie, I love you so much."

They made passionate love, but suddenly all Maria could say was, "We should've waited."

"We'll get married."

'They won't understand."

"Let's tell them of our intent. My parents will never throw me out of their house. We'll tell them that we want to be married."

Hand in hand, they found their way home, but now they feared for what they faced.

"Maybe, tomorrow, honey?"

"You're right. Tomorrow, we'll be thinking with a clear head, Johann."

So instead each of them went to their separate homes. Johann and Maria would continue to see each other as often as they could.

"We need to tell them, Johann."

"Should've done it before."

"We didn't. Mother keeps looking at me funny so I think she suspects. I have to say something. When do you want us to marry?"

"As soon as you and I can get our parent's permission."

"Let's ask them now."

They did just that.

The Classen's were mortified by their daughter's premarital pregnancy.

"You both should have waited. Didn't you even think of the shame we have to endure? You both know this is a very small town. I've heard you say so yourself about everybody being in everybody's business. Do you realize the shame we get to endure now?"

"Just give me permission to marry your daughter."

"That doesn't make anything go away. The answer is no, our daughter is too young. As I understand it, you Johann, are from the Conference Mennonites. You know we don't even agree on religion. How can we say yes to your marriage?

Her mother said, "Dear Maria, shouldn't you give your baby up for adoption? If you do, we will send you to another town to have your baby. Come back and no one will even know. We'll say we sent you away to boarding school. You'll be okay and your baby will get a good home. Please, would you consider doing that?"

"Never. I'm keeping my baby, Mother."

"If you really feel like that, Maria, we will probably have to leave our home. Move away."

"Why?"

"Small towns are never very forgiving for family dishonor."

"I want to marry Johann. Just allow me to marry him. If he doesn't go with us, I'm not moving with you."

"We'll see. His family might not like him coming with us."

"You heard me. If he doesn't go, neither do I."

Grandfather insisted, "We'll wait until you give birth and then we'll leave. It will be easier for you."

Johann's parents were just as devastated. "You know son, if Maria is keeping your baby, you need to take responsibility for her as well as your baby."

"I want to but Maria's parents are saying no. They are planning to leave for Manitoba after the baby is born. I want to go with them."

"Well, let your mother and I think about that. That will give us just enough time to go there as well. I'll set up land for both our families and let's build you a new home, for you and Maria. We'll make it work."

In was nine months when Maria went into labor. Labor was intense and hard for Maria, but the baby came. "I'm going to name him after his father, Johann." Maria hesitated, "When can Johann and I be married, Father?"

"As we said before, we are going to make the move first. You understand we can't stay here. You've heard people talk."

"I'm not strong enough to move yet."

"Yes, Maria. If you want Johann to have a normal life and not have everyone judging him because you are a single mother. That's just what we have to do."

Maria insisted, "Give us your consent to marry and then it won't matter anymore."

"If only it was that easy. We'll make the move and then talk."

Johann's family decided they would also make the move so that he could have a civil wedding when they would be relocated. Johann's father was a successful farmer and was able

to secure land for both Maria's family and his own. He would continue his business in the outlying areas of Winnipeg.
People in a small town would never look at Maria nor Johann the same. They might perhaps forgive Maria, but Johann would go unforgiven.

Maria was still weak from giving birth, but her condition was ignored and the plans to move became a reality as their buggies were packed. Food was prepared for the journey.

They started out during the evening hours while the town was peaceful and no one was stirring. They were making the move. It was important to cross over into Canada while the weather was still amenable. But most of all they had to keep up appearances.

"I think you are very wise in making this move." One of the town fathers told him. "I know how unforgiving this town is, especially with our Mennonite Conference."

He knew very well how intolerant people in their ethnic families were at the turn of the nineteenth century. It was common for everyone to know everyone's business and all the reasons for everything they did, or it had the buzz in the air to be so.

Johann and Maria were inseparable no matter how hard each of the families tried to keep them too busy in an attempt to curb their interest for one another.

"Thank you, Maria, for naming him after me. Do you know how much I love you?"

"I do."

"His name will be Johann Classen Penner."

While the weather was still travelable, the two families crossed over the Canadian border and on to Winnipeg, Manitoba, Canada, the nearest big City. It would be where they would be unknown.

However, shortly after childbirth and on arriving in Winnipeg, Maria became ill and then passed away. My father was then reared by another Penner family, however a Friesen family was chosen to be his financial Guardian.

Chapter **TWO**
My Family's Beginning

In his early 20s, my Father, Johann, later known as John, spent three years in Chicago to pursue an education in law in an attempt to become an attorney. Money became too tight for him to complete his endeavor. Instead he then chose to became a store owner in the City of Winnipeg. It was at this time he would meet the love of his live, Ana Unrau, my mother.

Many years later Mother told me the story.

"Will you marry me, Ana?" John was on his knees as Ana looked into his pleading eyes, for she knew he wanted her response to be 'Yes.'

"Yes, John! I've been waiting for you for most of my life."

"You were?"

"A gypsy in Russia told me the man I would marry would be tall, have blond hair and blue eyes. You have that. As I said, I've been waiting for you and I love you with all of my heart."

"Well, compared to your 4'11" I'd be tall alright."

"How tall are you?"

"6'1."

All John could say was, "When, how soon can we be married?"

"July 1."

"But that's a Sunday and it's Dominion Day."

"Of course! I want the entire Nation to Celebrate with us."

"They won't know that."

"Doesn't matter, they will be in celebration mode."

"But Ana, there isn't much time. Who can we get?"

"Our Pastor, Rev. C.N. Hiebert."

"But we are both from opposite Mennonite Denominations, I'm Conference and you're Brethren. Won't he object? It would probably be better if we just went to the justice of peace, the court house."

"Sorry, John. I want to be married in the Church. Let's just ask him."

The Pastor's response, "I'd be honored to be your officiating Pastor."

July 1 was the day they married, 1928. This was also only a year before the Great Depression began.

Work was sparse and understandably money was tight but John and Ana would have a total of six children. The Doctor had a long talk with Mother about having more children. "You know Ana, you've already had one miscarriage. You shouldn't have any more children."

"Whatever God gives me, I will have. I have enough love for all of them."

In spite of all the warnings of the Doctor, my mother had another baby boy, they named him Clarence. My parents wouldn't stop there.

On a particular school day, my Mother told me the story of what happened. Paulina, their eldest child, came home from school, crying in total agony and pain. She couldn't talk anymore and all that my parents could do was take her to the hospital where she would linger for a few weeks, then in May, 1938 she died from a brain aneurism.

That same year in November, when the snow was falling lightly, Ana went into labor and was taken to Winnipeg General hospital where she would give birth to a newborn baby girl, just six months after her firstborn daughter had passed away.

In 1938 women usually spent 10 days in the hospital recuperating, nursing and caring for her newborn. November was also the time of year when the Christmas Parade and Santa Claus would come to town, the exact day when I was born, November 17, 1938.

This is how I remember mother telling the story.

"What are you going to name your baby?" Our family Doctor inquired.

"I thought her name should be Linda Grace, Doctor."

"Linda Grace? Shouldn't her name be Diana? Your name is Ana, shouldn't you call her Diana? Wouldn't it sound better, Diana Elaine?"

"What do you think, John?" Mother, without hesitation said, "I think we'll do that then, John. Diana Elaine Penner, it does have a good sound to it."

My Father shrugged his shoulder, "I guess." This wasn't how Dad wanted it, after all he was my Father not the Doctor. That surely lit the light of Jealousy for him. By the time he got to the Registrar's office to complete the transaction, somehow my name escaped his memory. Later that day my Mother asked him.

"You did the name registration, John?"

"Sure."

"It is Diana Elaine, then?"

"I think her second name is Leuene, I think that's how I had them record her name."

"Well, then, Diana Leuene. That will be your choice, you got to name her middle name then."

"I think that's what I did."

When I needed to know my legal name for the first day starting school, I was told my name was Diana Leuene.

"When you go to school, they will ask you your name and where you live. You need to memorize that. Your name is Diana Leuene."

"Diana Leuene, I can remember that."

This was the first time I heard anyone say my middle name. *Well at least it's easy to spell but I still don't like it.* To me it sounded odd but what does a child say to her parents about the name they have chosen for her?

Chapter THREE
The Great Depression

I want to take a step back to catch up with the events in history. The Great Depression began on October 29, 1929, when the New York stock market crashed and lasted until 1939. The level of poverty was unprecedented due to unemployment. It accelerated the global economic collapse throwing Nations into the Great Depression, both in Canada and the U.S.

By 1933, nearly half of America's banks had failed, and unemployment was approaching 30 percent of the workforce or 15 million people. People were beginning to form lines, not for work, there wasn't any, but for food. It was common for men to hop onto boxcars for shelter, going from one town to another, begging for food. The lineup at Missions and soup kitchens was endless.

"Can I have a loaf of bread?"

"That'll be seven cents."

"I'm sorry Sir, I have no money, please can you put that on my account and I will pay just as soon as I find work."

This was heard all over the place. As a result, people began to default on their debt. For my Father, it meant people were unable to pay their bills they had accrued at his store.

"Ana, I don't think I can keep the store open anymore. All the money I manage to take in, is used to buy supplies for resale, there is nothing left. As a matter of fact, I don't even have enough money to pay my suppliers. There is no more profit in keeping the store open. No one can pay for what they need to buy."

The result? My Father closed his store.

He joined the Army reserves but was never called to serve overseas because of the size of our family. Finally, he worked for Dominion Bridge, a Canadian Steel bridge constructor in Winnipeg making parts for the War effort. He would work two shifts. The early morning, come home and sleep for a couple of hours and then work another shift just to meet the needs of our family.

"I'm working all I can to keep up with the medical expenses. I don't know what to do."

"What do you want me to do? I can go to work."

"Tell me, what can you do?"

"Sewing factory. My friends are doing it."

"We have too many kids. We can't afford a baby sitter."

"If you work the night shift, I'll work the day shift. Maybe you can sleep while the kids are in school. You just need to be here when they come home from school. By that time, I'll be home from work, make dinner and you can go to work."

My mother tried that but it wasn't working. "Don't think this is going to work, John. You're exhausted by watching the kids and then when I come home, I'm tired and have to make dinner so you can go to work. I'm so tired I can't even sleep anymore."

"How do we pay all the medical bills?"

"I don't know, John. What can we do but trust God?"

My Journey on the Road to Emmaus　　　　　　　　　　　Diana E. Linn

Chapter **FOUR**
Sometimes it Hurts

I remember standing next to Calvin as he rested his leg on the footstool in our living room. He showed me how swollen his leg really was.

"It really hurts."

"It really looks like it must hurt badly. You need to tell Mom and Dad. They'll know what to do for you."

I felt bad for him. The first thing they said to him was, "Who pushed you today? What did they do, fight at school again? I know they think we are German because we called our Terrier Fritz. They kicked the dog until he died. Now they're doing it to you."

The reason the dog died is debatable. We always fed him chicken bones and I suppose that might be why he didn't make it. Yet, my parents were convinced that the swollen knee Calvin was experiencing had to be due to the scuffles the boys would have at school. It had to be from all the bumps and bruises kids get while playing and, in their opinion, people were prejudiced. It had to be somebody's fault. That is how it always was even when I became ill, it had to be because I didn't do something right. I probably wasn't careful enough and maybe got too cold some of the time, but it's my fault?

It was 1941 when my brother Calvin was diagnosed with bone cancer. In those days, amputating a person's leg was the medical answer to curing cancer. Just cut cancer out.
However, that isn't how life worked for Calvin.
Soon the time came when the Doctor asked Calvin, "Is there anything you really want to do or see?"
"You're asking me? I'd love to see Vancouver. With all the pictures I've seen, it must be absolutely beautiful. And then the ocean, to see the water. Not only that but the mountains, like Grouse Mountain. I've only seen pictures of it but is one of the North Shore Mountains of the Pacific Range in the District Municipality of North Vancouver. I'd love to see all that. Do you think I ever will?"
"I don't know Calvin. I'll talk to your parents. See what they say."
My parents discussed it at length. How would all that be possible?
"John, what do you think about moving to Vancouver?"
"That would be good, Ana but there aren't even places for rent in Vancouver according to all the Newspaper reports. Where would we stay?"
"My Father is there. He has an apartment, he'll let us stay with him."
"But, Ana, there are too many of us to do that, he has a one-room studio apartment."

"Trust me, John. There'll be a place for us. We just have to be there to get the house."

He knew if Mother said it would be so, it probably would be. Then, realizing the time was limited for Calvin and as it was Calvin's desire to see the Port of Vancouver, they made the decision to move. Both my parents knew very well, that the Doctor's prediction of two years would be all he had to live. This would be his last wish, compounded by the fact that I was suffering from Asthma, our family Doctor recommended the milder climate. It should be a good move both for both of us.

Vancouver is not only a City located near the mouth of the Fraser River but it is also protected by Vancouver Island. Unusual for a Canadian city, Vancouver has relatively mild winters with little snow. The cold air from the Arctic that sweeps over the rest of Canada in winter is unable to reach Vancouver as easily because of the Rocky Mountains.

Combine the lack of Arctic air with the mildness of Vancouver's location on the shores of the Pacific Ocean and it's not surprising that Vancouver is the warmest of Canada's major metropolitan cities in winter.

Snow depths of greater than a quarter of an inch are seen on about 10 days each year in Vancouver compared with about 65 days in Toronto. Vancouver has one of the wettest and foggiest climates of Canada's cities. At times, in winter, it can seem that the rain will never stop.

Compensating for the wet winters, Vancouver usually enjoys excellent summer weather characterized by very pleasant, warm days with abundant sunshine. Although I recall, trying to plan for picnics as a kid was always scheduled depending on weather conditions. Never an arrangement made in stone. We'd never know for sure whether our plans would actually happen. We learned to have many group picnics inside instead of outdoors.

Vancouver also differs from most other Canadian cities in that it has a genuine spring. In many Canadian cities, it often seems that warm, summer weather replaces frigid, winter weather in a matter of a very few weeks or even days.

Vancouver has a western maritime climate, causing its weather to be changeable throughout the year and therefore is less windy than most other Canadian cities.[1]

Dad had been able to secure a transfer to the Vancouver Division of Dominion Bridge. The move was now in place.

It was a pleasant change from the long train trip all the way from Manitoba, along the flat prairie and then through the Rocky Mountains to Vancouver. I remember, my mother didn't do so well. She was worried and, on the way, had a heart attack. This terrified my Father. He was beside himself. But, as always, my mother came through and the next stop was Vancouver.

I was about to turn 4 years of age, yet, I remember like it was yesterday, getting off at the train station. First, my parents put all our belongings into storage near the station.

"It's okay, kids, we have to put our stuff into storage until we can find a place to live."

---

[1] Living in Canada, online

"That'll be easier." Mother didn't want the worry of keeping track of all our stuff. "There are always lockers we can use here at the train station. Everybody does that these days."

"It has to be big enough to hold all our stuff."

It didn't take but a few minutes to locate the right area at the train station to make the arrangements. Then we walked in search of Grandfather's Apartment, but it seemed my parents knew exactly where to go.

"Okay, kids. This seems to be the right street. Let's ask someone."

Like any other man, Dad would say, "We'll find it."

Just as normal, my brother Joe would excitedly say, "Here is the address, this must be it." So, along with the rest of us, the excitement escalated as we entered the apartment. I remember the stairs in front of us, only a few would bring us to the mailboxes on the right.

"Look, kids, his name is Abram Unrau, it's on those mailboxes." My mother didn't have to say that twice. From there the steps turned to the left with Grandfather's door on the first landing.

"Here it is with his apartment number."

My Mother would insist, "You must be quiet, we can't cause a commotion. There are other people that live here and they won't want to hear a bunch of kids making noises. We don't want to be kicked out or worse yet, have my Father kicked out, then we would all be homeless."

Instantly, Grandfather opened the door. Surely, he could hear us come up the wooden stairs. There it was, a small one-room apartment with light that came in from the 4' x 4' window. I looked around and saw everything in one sweep. it was just as Dad had said it would be. A potbelly stove right smack in the middle. Though I was only 3' tall, with outstretched hands, I could easily reach the chain to turn the light on and off, the only light in the room. The floors were wooden and if we weren't careful, they would creek.

It wasn't long before my mother prepared what little food was available and made dinner for us all. Since it was already dark at this time of year, it wasn't long before my mother laid out sheets for us to sleep on the floor. We must have been really tired because I remember thinking, that floor is hard, how am I ever going to be able to sleep? Then I remember waking up with the rising sunlight pouring through the window in the morning with no ill effects.

The next morning, my Dad and brothers checked the newspaper and, sure enough, there was a house a few blocks from my Grandfather's apartment. Just as my mother predicted. The house was being vacated by a Japanese family selling their home since they were being relocated because of the war. My parents bought that house, furniture and all. Within days we were living in a large 6-bedroom house. Room enough for all of us. The address I remember well, 1519 W. 3rd Avenue but this was now October of 1942.

By 1942, World War II was in progress and food began to be rationed, items such as tea, coffee, sugar, butter, and mechanical parts were sparse. I remember the coupons we were given and watched Mother work out a plan to make it all work.

Those were the days we were given books with tickets to use so that we would be able to buy certain portions of food items on certain days.

"Today's the day we can go and get some peanut butter. Want to come with me?"

I remember getting bored as we stood there and lost concentration on where I was. This is when I realized I didn't have a sense of direction and could easily get lost. My mother was there, just a few feet ahead of me but that didn't matter, I couldn't see her at first, but then I did.

But it was wartime, we were in the middle of a world war. On June 20, 1942, a Japanese submarine surfaced and shelled the Lighthouse at Estevan Point on the West Coast of Vancouver Island, on the Hesquiat Peninsula.[2] I remember very well when my parents said,

"We're being bombed." We all rushed to the back window to look out to see the plumes of smoke go up. We were all aware of it, we could see it, but still, it wasn't very close to us.

My mother would advise us, "If anyone ever asks you, we are not German. We are of Dutch descent. Both your Father and I are originally Dutch, there is no other blood in our vanes."

My mother was adamant about that. "Furthermore, we are not related to anyone with black hair." I think she meant we weren't Jewish either. This was somewhat strange because my Grandfather had black hair. It wasn't too visible because he was mostly white-haired already.

---

[2] Wikipedia, Estevan Point, June 20, 1942

As it happened, we were neighbors to the famous actress Yvonne DeCarlo's grandparents. Yvonne De Carlo was a Canadian-American actress, dancer, and singer. A brunette with blue-grey eyes, who became an internationally famous Hollywood film star in the 1940s and 1950s, making several recordings, and later acted on television and stage. She was born September 1, in Vancouver, Canada and died January 8, 2007, in Los Angeles, California.[3]

Mother would visit often with the aging grandmother. I would always accompany her on these occasions as they enjoyed a cup of tea together. Often the elderly lady would offer to give Mother items of interest but mother would always refuse. She would insist Yvonne's Grandmother needed to leave her things to her family. Finally, mother accepted an old desk for me from Yvonne. It was a desk she had as a child when living with her Grandmother. We kept that desk in our home until I finally moved out into my own apartment.

We settled in Vancouver but very soon Calvin was admitted to the hospital and at the age of twelve, just two years after we had moved to Vancouver, he passed away. Then in less than two years later, my grandfather, Abram Unrau, passed away at the age of 71. I was now 7 years old.

---

[3] Wikipedia

For me, attending school wasn't to be in the cards because of my illness and as a result, I was homeschooled for my first two years of elementary education.

My mother would lay all the books on the table and tell me to read the instructions.

I'd say, "What is this word? What does it mean?"

"I don't know. Just copy everything on this paper. Eventually, you'll know what it says."

I did that over and over again. No one would tell me, no one would teach me. I remember I had to write a letter to the school my lessons were coming from. I still don't know how I did that because I would copy word for word. It would take me hours.

My father would teach me Math and how to write, but not how to print. He figured I could bypass that. It would be unnecessary in the scheme of things.

I would watch my Dad draft the houses he had been hired to build.

"Are you interested in doing these drawing, Diane?" (I never understood why he would never call me Diana).

"I'd love to. Do you think I can do it good enough for you?"

"Try it."

I did and from then on Dad would have me do his architectural drawing for the houses he built. He showed me how they should look and what each part meant. He would use them to get permits from the city.

Still, in my mind, it didn't compute. No one saw the missing links but then Mother wasn't a teacher and didn't have a command of the English language.

The area we lived in had become industrialized as the businesses began replacing homes with shops. Most families had already moved to the suburbs in search of a better environment. We had factories on either side of our house. A machine shop on one side and the Laundry across the alleyway. The train was a few yards behind our house. The noise never did bother us, it had become routine. Part of life's story, it would always be there.

Often the men working in the shop next to our house would offer to take us on rides through the city as they delivered parts to other businesses.

We would spend many days at False Creek Beach just a few blocks away from our house. We could feel the cool breeze from the water and in the nearby park, escaping the pollution from the factories around our house. Though I am fearfully afraid of the water, I would wade just a few feet from the shore under mother's watchful eye.

Chapter **FIVE**
Illness in Turmoil

After my brother and Grandfather had already passed away, I did get Chicken Pox. I remember my parents had to darken the rooms so that no sunlight could touch my skin. They said, if they didn't do that, we could even go blind.

After that incident I attempted to attend public school but only made it for one day when my Asthma came back in a furry. Mother assumed it could likely be from the chicken-pox, that had lowered my immune system.

There was a knock on our door. My mother answered.

"We understand that you are keeping your daughter home from attending School. You know it is mandatory for her to be allowed to attend school."

"She is ill, unable to attend."

They came in to see me and sure enough, they understood so they made arrangements for materials to be sent so that I could begin to learn at home. From there it was homeschooling over the next couple of years.

On one of my bad days, I was sleeping on the sofa when I heard my mother say to her friends that had dropped by to see how I was doing. My mother said, "I have given her up to the Lord. My prayer is that God would take her home. We've tried everything. The Doctor gives her medicine but she can't keep it down."

I heard every word she said and I knew I was in trouble. I prayed, *God if you will let me live, when someone can show me the way, I will follow you for the rest of my life.*

The ladies had tea with mother and shortly thereafter, left. Within just a few minutes I heard another knock at the door. This time It was the Fuller Brush salesman.

Mother answered, "I don't think I need anything this time, Sir."

He couldn't help but notice me lying on the sofa, when he said, "Is there something wrong with your daughter?"

"She suffers from Asthma and there isn't anything anyone can do for her."

"Here, use this. It's a pump you can use to spray the medicine orally into her mouth. This is the name of the drug you can get in any drug store." He handed the piece of paper with the name of the drug on it.

Mother immediately went to the corner drug store and was able to get the medicine from the pharmacy and did as he advised. Immediately, I sat up. I was well.

"I'm hungry."

For the first time in years, I could eat normally, do anything other child could do.

Chapter SIX
The Invitation

If I would listen to my brothers, my family all allegedly attended Church while living in Winnipeg. However, by the time of my birth, living life had gotten in the way of attending church. My mother and father grew fatigued in caring for the family, and as a result, my parents no longer considered themselves churchgoers. This made it impossible for me to know I was born into a Christian family, though my parents were caring, upright, and good living people.

In later years, my mother often told us how God had intervened in so many ways.

"Your Father and I didn't always know where our next meal would come from. We would pray in the morning. He would go to work. By the time I was going to make dinner again, I went to the cupboards. Right there, the cupboards were filled with canned food and more. Everything I needed to make dinner with." That was a Devine Miracle ... coming from God was the only answer. There just was no other answer.

"God has answered, Ana," my father would say.

Mother told us when they had first married my Dad and she read the Scriptures and prayed together on a daily basis until life took a turn for the worst. She tells the story about them wanting to start a church meeting in their home but because my father was Conference Mennonite and Mother was Mennonite Brethren, the church wouldn't approve. Finally, the Church and the reading of the Bible became forbidden in our household. Life had broken my Dad. He no longer wanted anything to do with God.

It was now 1946, Dad was at work on the night shift, as always. We were sitting at the dining room table.

"Look at the Cat, Mother, what's wrong with the Cat?"

My brother Joe said, "She's running in circles."

"Now she just stares." Then the rumble. Our 110 year-old-house shook, my brother Joe ran down the back stairs.

Mother shouted to him, "Don't do that, Joe. Just stand in the doorway." Joe was already standing on the ground.

Then, just as suddenly, it was over. We were terrified but we followed down the stairs though mother was insistent that we should be cautious of the old stairs as we descended down.

My mother would say, "I think the house will be okay. The stairs seem stable enough. We should be okay."

"Isn't that a deep hole in the roadway?"

Joe said, "That wasn't there before the earthquake."

We just stood there gazing at the indentation with my three brothers and me. The huge pothole was about 10-feet-wide in the alleyway between our house and the laundry. This was the first earthquake I'd ever experienced. We were terrified. What did it mean?

Apparently, the earth is divided into huge pieces, called tectonic plates and when they slip past or under one another releasing stress, it causes the ground to move and shake. For Vancouver, the strait of Juan de Fuca plates move under the American plate in the Cascadia Subduction Zone where they cause megathrust quakes. These can register greater than 9.0. Fortunately, in 1946, it wasn't as serious for us. Apparently, there were 21 earthquake events that year that measured at least 7.0. As reported, a very busy earthquake year.[4]

It was at this time mother wanted to give comfort to each of her children, so that evening while my father was working the night shift, my mother pulled her Bible out and asked my brothers to read it out loud since my mother couldn't read the English language very well. Dad had promised he would help her with the English but then didn't.

However, in our home our mother tongue was Dutch, we understood it very well but my siblings and I spoke English. Recently and in the writing of my memoirs, I've been re-reading some of my mother's writings where she says she was fluent in seven different languages but as the years went by, she could now only speak fluently in Dutch, Russian and German but had to struggle with English.

My eldest brother refused my mother's request to read Scriptures because my Dad had forbidden the Bible in our home

---

[4] City of Vancouver. Earthquake facts, learn the risks

and he would never disobey his father. But Joe, curious to see what God had to say, read the Word of God aloud to all of us. We sat and listened. I remember thinking, how can we know what all this means? We aren't allowed to talk about God.

We sat there and listened to what God was saying. My thoughts were, *if you allow me, God, I want to know you.*

Chapter **SEVEN**
The Move

With Dad working many overtime hours, my parents soon were able to purchase land from the municipality in North Burnaby, a suburb of Vancouver, named after Burnaby Lake. Apparently, Robert Burnaby had explored the region in late 1859.

In the first 30 to 40 years after its incorporation, the growth of Burnaby was influenced by its location between the expanding urban centers of Vancouver and New Westminster.

It first served as a rural agricultural area supplying nearby markets. Later, it served as an important transportation corridor between Vancouver, the Fraser Valley, and the Interior, and continues to do so.[5]

It was now in the mid-40s when my father began building our new home in hopes that they would be able to sell the Vancouver property to complete the building. By the time they were able to sell, a highway had been built on the edge of our

---

[5] Wikipedia, the Free Encyclopedia

land in Vancouver and as a result, they could only sell for the value of the land.

My brothers and I, along with my mother spent many days at the new location helping in any way possible while my father built our house. On one particular occasion, a young couple stopped by to talk with my Father as he was building our house.

"Sir, we would like very much if you could build a house for us."

Dad, said, "I'm busy, maybe in a few months when I'm finished here."

"But we just want a one-room house. We think you could probably do it in a short period of time."

Both my parents discussed it and decided maybe they could use the extra money and put it into the building of our house. He did and completed it within a few months but as I remember, the young couple discovered they didn't anymore have the money to pay for the labor. My mother would then be the collector for my Dad. She was unrelenting by visiting over and over again until they finally paid their debt.

Mill Strike

By the time my father started back on our home, a mill strike took place and as a result, we ended up moving into an incomplete home for a time. We lived in that house into my early adult years, but it was always under construction.

_____

God isn't silent, His answer for me was on the way before I even asked.

We were now settled in North Burnaby into our home when life took another twist in circumstances. From there, life was abruptly interrupted.

It had been a difficult year for my family but it was how God brought us back to reality. On one of those pleasant west coast Vancouver Indian summer evenings we, as a family, walked along the wooden sidewalk on Hastings Street in North Burnaby. The Salvation Army's band was out front of their Hall (we would call it a Chapel) playing and singing.

We were among many people who had stopped to be entertained. They shared a quick message from God's Word and then approached my parents inviting us to attend their services.

The Salvation Army, being a Protestant Christian International charitable organization may have been of some interest to both my parents for at this point they knew they needed someone's help. It was then, my parents had decided we could attend Sunday School on Sunday afternoons at their Hall.

I remember that Christmas. I asked my mother if we were going to have a Christmas tree.

"I don't think we can do that this year."

"I'll decorate the tree if we could get one. Don't we have any decorations?"

"We do. I have a lot of really small ones.

It wasn't long before Clarence brought home the tree. He had been working at the bowling alley's fish & Chip restaurant. He bought the tree, and I began to decorate.

We attended the Salvation Army and as always, the Salvation Army had a big Christmas celebration where Santa Claus comes to visit and bring gifts to all the children.

My Mother insisted, "We will all go to the program tonight but I don't want any of you to be disappointed. Others will likely receive gifts but we've only just started going there, they don't even know your names, so I don't expect you'll get anything."

We walked through the snow to the Hall, all five of us. The sidewalks were slippery and as a result, every step had to be measured so as not to fall.

We sat down on some of the empty chairs and tried to join in with the music as they sang Rudolph the Red Nose Rain deer and other secular songs. I remember being surprised but enjoyed it along with everyone else.

Jolly Old Santa appeared, making his grand entrance from the back of the building. One by one he called the names of the children and gave each a gift.

"Elmer, Joe, Clarence and Diana." They called our names.

We looked at our Mother. "Are they calling us?"

"Go ahead, you can accept what they give you but don't open them."

We accepted our gifts and held onto them and didn't open a one although we watched the other children open their gifts.

On Christmas morning, we all had some kind of a gift. We opened our gifts. Some had been broken but we had gifts.

"Mine's broken."

"There's a missing part on mine."

Mother said, "At least they remembered to give you all a gift."

It was there, at the Salvation Army Sunday School that I earned my first New Testament for memorizing the Beatitudes. Oh, did I say I couldn't read? My brothers read to me and I memorized. That's right, I was being homeschooled and taught by my mother, but remember she couldn't read English.

However, since we had moved from our Vancouver location, my Asthma subsided, probably because we were no longer living near the factories and all the pollution. My health had changed for the better, so it had become time for me to start public school. I started attending Rosser Avenue elementary school.

I would be turning nine in the fall but had missed the first two semesters of school.

I'll never forget the first day at school for me. Mother had explained to the second-grade teacher how badly she had taught me but she felt that with other students to learn from, I would learn more easily.

Mother left.

Sitting in class, the teacher said to me, "Let's try this word."

I could read. Surprise, I didn't know but I had been reading bit by bit all along. Along with the teaching of phonics, it took me one semester to catch up and by the end of the school year, I was reading well and quickly moved up into the next grade.

My Journey on the Road to Emmaus   Diana E. Linn

I remember that first day at school. My brothers were supposed to wait for me after class and walk me home. I came out of school and they were nowhere to be found. I frantically looked around and tried to remember how we had all walked together in the morning. As it was, I actually took another route home but quite suddenly I started to see the familiar buildings and streets. I was five blocks from home but I did find my way.

The next year began as a good year but then suddenly there was an outbreak of Scarlet Fever. Quarantined signs went up on houses all over our neighborhood. I came home with the earaches, and whatever else happens. My mother didn't want those signs on the door of our house. As a result, she refused to call a Doctor. They couldn't afford that anyhow.

As a result, it took me two weeks to get well and then from there I had the joint pain that would follow me the rest of my life. That part would have happened in spite of what my parents did but now I had missed two weeks of school. To my parents, I just needed to get well. To me I missed too much of school and didn't know how I would catch up with my history classes. I would then struggle with that subject. Other classes were easy though.

By now, my intent was to become an officer in the Salvation Army. You see, I do whatever I do, all the way.

My brother Clarence was invited to join the Salvation Army band practice. I begged my mother to allow me to join the band as well. My mother had to do a little arm twisting to get me into the band. It was an all-male band. I wanted to learn to play so badly and knew that playing a wind instrument was good for lung exercising. Finally, they condescended to allow me to play the Baritone horn while my brother played the Trombone.

However, we practiced forever but never performed anywhere.

The lady Lieutenants would ask me from time to time that they had intended to ask me if I could play such and such a song with them for the afternoon service.

"I've been practicing that and all the other songs in the songbook with the Baritone horn at home a lot."

Nothing ever transpired in that situation, just encouraging talk, I'm sure. Little did they know, I was playing in the public-school band on the side without ever asking if I had permission to use the instrument at the school.

One of the boys in the band inquired of the bandmaster, "Sir, when will we be good enough to perform somewhere?"

His answer was, "There is a summer camp coming up in just a few weeks that you will need to attend. It's very intensive but you get to learn everything and will be playing very well by the time the two weeks are up. Then we will be performing."

Of course, it was for boys only. That clearly pulled me out of playing in the Band and surely, they realized that allowing me to be a part in practicing for a time would then come to an end. Soon that had become history for me. My brother wasn't interested in attending the specialized camp since camping was never in his DNA nor mine. Possibly, not even any of our family.

My Journey on the Road to Emmaus　　　　　　　　　　Diana E. Linn

Chapter **EIGHT**
The Call

It was a short time after we had started attending the Salvation Army, the call came loud and clear for me, there was no mistaking the call. To me, the voice was audible, clear and by name, but I was only a child.

I inquired of my Mother if she had called my name. She said, "No," two separate times. It came again and then I knew it had to be God. It was first and foremost a call to himself. Here was my quandary, I wasn't ten years old yet.

I remember. My eldest brother Elmer came asking if my mother had called him.

She said no. And shortly after that, we were discussing this phenomenon with the consensus that we were hearing words caused by electrical currents that ran through the atmosphere and from time to time, we would hear things.

For me, it was very real and then I remembered, I had made that promise to God. As I recalled, he had answered immediately.

"My daughter, I'm calling you to be my child."

"Lord, I remember very well. I said if you would get me through my illness and if you would show me the way, I would follow you and I meant it."

God hadn't forgotten my promise either. Now he was calling. My reply? You would've expected me to say, "Yes, Yes, God, I'm ready. Instead, I said, "No, God. Not now. I'm well now, I'm okay. I want to make it on my own, prove I can do this. I really don't want to be a Tin Soldier and just submit to people who should know better or should know right from wrong."

He waited.

However, I did have one major problem for I knew I had to be *good*.

The being good dilemma was instilled into my being from the day I was born. You see, my parents insisted my sister was too good to live. As I said earlier, she passed away the same year I was born, just prior to my birth. That wouldn't mean a lot except that I was told we would have been twins in every way but for one thing, we were nine years apart. Nonetheless, no one in my family would let me forget that I was a replacement for Paulina. God persisted to show me my inadequacies, that I really couldn't proceed on my own and still be *good*.

Then a family incident happened. My brother Joe was good at relentlessly taunting me. He would never give up. I finally had enough, grabbed a hammer throwing it at him. The hammer hit him in the leg. He went off crying to the neighbors and I went back into our house and prayed for God to forgive me. I never intended to hurt anyone but I did. It was then I asked God to forgive me, come into my life and be my Savior. He did just that as He promised.

It was customary with the Salvation Army to have a call of acceptance for Salvation every Palm Sunday. The invitation was given that very next Sunday and I went forward, and acknowledged my need for accepting Christ as my Savior on Palm Sunday, 1947, in that small Salvation Army Hall. From that day forward, with all my fears, I knew God was with me every step of the way. I soon learned that all three of my brothers testified at that time that they had accepted Jesus as their Savior as well. As of the writing of my memoirs, all three of my brothers have since gone to be with Jesus.

I learned a lot in the Salvation Army for the years I attended. It was customary for them to teach New Testament stories every Sunday. I had no problem hearing them again and again, in the repetition. It seemed it was all that they had to share with us as children.

On the lighter side of life, my parents would often entertain our neighbors and the lady Lieutenants from the Salvation Army for a dinner party at our house. Mother prepared a lavish dinner for our guests with her famous homemade rolls that she had developed a secret recipe for with all the meat and potatoes you could want. On this occasion when our guests were more than halfway through their dinner, when one of them commended my mother for all she had done.
"This is a very delicious dinner you prepared for us, Ana."

Dad said, "It tastes just like chicken, you can't tell the difference."

Someone asked, "It isn't chicken?"

"You wouldn't know this is rabbit meat."

I watched as one of our male guests had been eating on a leg, still in his mouth that he thought was a chicken leg. As soon as my Father said that, he dropped it on his plate and declared he was too full to eat any more. One by one the guests said, "I think I've had plenty. I'm going to have to leave it at that."

Now you must understand, I was always taught that even though these Rabbits were my pets and I cared for them every day, they would all eventually become dinner. My eldest brother didn't quite agree with that. He had a pet rooster that became dinner and it took him years to eat chicken no matter how it was prepared.

Chapter **NINE**
Walking in the Call

I had never been short of friends while attending school but Pat and I would walk home from High School many times together and she had apparently been attending a girl's club at Capitol Hill Alliance church up on Capitol hill in North Burnaby. She invited me to attend with her.

"I don't know if I can go with you."

"Ask your mother."

"But I never ask my parents anything."

"Just ask her. Just so you know, the crafts we do are a lot of fun but Mrs. Hauge does a lot of talking and Bible teaching. She likes us to memorize a lot of Scriptures."

I told Mother it was an Alliance Church. To my amazement, she was pleased. I attended and found that there was so much of God's word I didn't know and hadn't learned yet. Mrs. Hauge was indeed a patient but insistent Bible teacher. It was all that my girlfriend had said it would be.

As time went on, we were invited to participate in a *game plan*. If we would attend Sunday School and Church regularly for a quarter (3 months) and memorize a series of Scriptures (we had to repeat each of the Scripture as we added another verse every Sunday), we would win an Airplane ride with Air Canada as they were offering 20-minute advertising flights around the city. Of course, if there's a challenge, I'm always in. There were at least 15 of us who had successfully completed the challenge. My mother didn't object until I was about to board the airplane. I came home with a letter that at least one of my parents had to sign.

"Diana, I don't think you should take that airplane ride."

"Why?"

"It's too dangerous. I don't want you to go."

"But Mother, I worked hard for this, I worked really hard. I want to go."

"I don't have a good feeling about it."

"It's going to be okay," my Dad insisted.

And so, I did. Mother wasn't pleased but I did it anyhow. As I recall, the Pilot made the circle around the city pointing out the landscape from the sky. Mother was deathly afraid that the plane would crash. I was young but with my Dad's authorization, I was able to fly. Nonetheless, I enjoyed the 20-minute flight around the city.

As a result, I became a regular Church attender. Then God began to feed me His Word through Pastor Hauge. He was an amazing Pastor that knew the Word. I soaked it up like a sponge and at the time I would remember every word he spoke to us, every sermon he preached, word for word.

    I had been attending the Capitol Hill Alliance for just a short time when my brother Elmer came home, unhappy.

    Mother asked, "What's wrong, Elmer?"

    "The Bible study at the Salvation Army isn't anything about the Bible. They are only teaching the Do's and Don'ts about the Salvation Army. I just wanted to study the Bible with them. I'm beginning to believe what Joe said."

    "What did Joe say?"

    "You remember, when we all collected door to door for money and when we met the quota, they told everyone to continue collecting and to tell people we had not met the quota yet. They wanted us to collect more. They asked us to lie."

    "Elmer, tell me what's really bothering you?" Mother knew Elmer was miffed with all the Salvation Army stood for.

    "They want me to date one of the girls in the Salvation Army."

    "I take it, they're match-making a love affair for you when you aren't exactly ready for a commitment."

    "That's it. I'm no longer going to attend church. I'm going to be a woman-hater from now on." He had enough of everything. For him, it was now over. He would become a devoted bachelor.

    "I agree with you on one account. The Salvation Army doesn't practice the ordinances of the Church because they consider themselves to be an Army, not a Church. I really didn't want you to become an Officer with them."

    "I'm quitting everything. It's over."

"I don't think you should do that either. You are the oldest of all your siblings. You need to be an example to them. It's your responsibility."

I listened to Mother and thought this might be a good time to say something. "Okay, Elmer, do what you want but if you quit now, so will I. How do you like that?"

Mother said, "Why don't you attend Capitol Hill Alliance where Diana is attending?" I wasn't about to follow through with that threat but I figured if it would keep my brother on track, what hurt would that do? My call wasn't dependent on him or anyone else but if he thought so and it kept him following Jesus, why not? The end result in this case benefited the cause. For the sake of a soul?

As a result of all this, he began attending Capitol Hill Alliance. After that, he and my youngest brother Clarence and I were attending my church. My brother Joe had already joined the Navy, he wasn't around.

A member of the congregation asked, "Who is that guy? He comes in right after the offering and then leaves right after the benediction. We never have a chance to even greet him. Who is he?"

"That, my friend, is my youngest brother, Clarence."

"Why does he do that?"

"Who knows, but he is my brother." He was regular at it, every Sunday. He never missed a service.

My parents were very pleased that we were attending Capitol Hill Alliance, but unless I was able to convince them to attend with us on special occasions, they weren't there. Strange as it may sound, I still didn't know they were Christians until a tragedy was beginning to unfold in our family and I heard my mother say, "Oh, my God. I'm a Christian Mother and this is happening to me?" Then I knew she was a Christian.

My Mother had gotten everyone's attention because of this incident. She told them she had made a decision.

"From now on, I want everyone, that means you, Dad, and all of you kids have to promise to attend Capitol Hill Alliance every Sunday for a complete year. You will begin to see what a difference it will make in our home life."

That is exactly what happened. For one whole year, our family attended church and I can honestly testify, it made a total difference in our family behavior.

Would they continue this trend? Unfortunately, my father would not. He said, "My commitment was for only one year and I kept that commitment. That's enough church for me."

The Rock of Ages Quartet came to our Church and I convinced my parents to attend as well. They were pleased and did attend that special event.

Music, of course, always speaks to me so when the Rock of Ages Quartet presented a challenge, I accepted, though not publicly.

My parents, mostly my Father, on the other hand, felt that church was for Children, not for adults. Adults, he felt, should already know right from wrong and live a good Christian life. It wasn't a necessity to always be in Church.

The ashes of my life were beginning to ignite. I was beginning to put speed in my step for Jesus. I heard people complaining that students could no longer be seen with a Bible at school. I heard that, but I said, watch me. Along with my books, I packed my Bible, it now had to be one of them. No one disputed my decision. I declared it a myth. As a matter of fact, one of my teachers publicly commended me for doing that with some class discussion.

At this point of my life, I was literally on fire for the Lord. Soon I discovered my eldest brother was not only attending other Christian events, but he was always out on *skid row* handing out tracts. Before long I was persuaded that I should come to some of his studies and so I did. I'm not so sure he liked that. he wanted some time without his family, especially his baby sister.

Then I said, "I want to go to *Youth for Christ* on Saturday night

"You can't come."

"Why?'

"You'd have to be an usher."

"I can learn to do that. Someone just has to show me." And so, I attended and became an usher at the Saturday night *Youth for Christ*.

It wasn't long before I met other youth who shared the same desires.
this was the beginning of my heeding the call to become a missionary and from that day forward I planned to work toward that goal.

My Journey on the Road to Emmaus   Diana E. Linn

While in Junior high school, one of our assignments was to financially figure out what we might like to do upon graduation. My plan was designed to becoming a missionary with Africa as my focus point. As a result, my student counselor concurred with my ambition giving me advice on what classes should be of interest to me. I did follow through with that, knowing full well I'd never be able to afford Bible College.

At this point I decided not to question the future and just do what I could from where I was. As a result, I began to enroll in every class I could manage and be allowed to have. The end result had to be what the Lord would want. He knows the end from the beginning, not me. My class presentation went into great detail graphically with pictures to show how to evangelize. As a result, my school counselor made it obvious to me that she was also a believer.

I followed that advice and plan. As a result, by the time I was in Senior High School I was cramming all the subjects I could take into those next years of my high school education.

In my mid-teenage years, the late Rev. Peter Wittenberg, missionary to Germany came to be our interim Pastor at Capitol Hill Alliance. He challenged the youth to witness the Gospel to friends and acquaintances. I started to do that but somehow, I still didn't really know what I was doing, so I would invite the unchurched friends to my church. The church didn't exactly appreciate this.

"Who are these kids?"

"Friends from school. I invited them to come."

"But they aren't even church people."

"I know, that's why I invited them."

I felt I was doing what Pastor Wittenberg suggested. Isn't that what he meant? Isn't that what Jesus would do? Who knew the church wouldn't like that aspect of missionary work? Of course, my unchurched friends became more aware of that than I did.

While attending high school I discussed with my many friends what type of future we would want.

I remember in our Art class, "When do you think Jesus will come back again?"

"I'll bet by the year 2000, he has to have come back by then. Isn't that 2000 years since Jesus died on the cross?"

"That has to be the time."

"But the Bible says we won't know when that day is."

"Now everyone is talking about landing on the moon. I don't believe that's possible. That means we would contaminate the universe, that's bringing sin to the moon. God surely won't allow that."

On one such occasion, we discussed what type of man we might marry.

"Who do you think you'll marry someday, Diana?"

"It's like this, Shirley, I will never marry a farmer for one thing."

"Why?"

"I just know. He also cannot be a Tom, Dick or Harry and especially not a man with a name like John. His name will have to be Bert and he will have to have a crew cut."

"Are you serious?"

"I am really serious. Not only that he will have had to have a track record of at least ten years of following Jesus. No way will I marry someone who says they'll attend Church and then after you marry, they don't. He has to prove himself before I ever meet him and am willing to say I do."

"That's funny, Diana. There is a guy in the 11th grade at our school. His name is Bert and he has a crew-cut. He owns a couple of horses as well. But, you know, I don't really think he is a Christian. He certainly doesn't act like it."

"Well, what can I say. I'm not interested unless he knows the Lord."

That was the conversation. I heard no more and had put him out of my mind. I wasn't ready for a real commitment anyhow.

It must have been mating season. It seems a lot of my friends were already dating and that's likely why I was asked by them, "Have you found anyone to date, yet?"

"Yeah, no. I'm not sure I'm interested in anyone. My parents have strong feelings on everything. I think I'll wait until I turn 18 when I don't have to have permission."

"You must have seen Stanley around. He walks to school probably about the same time as you do in the mornings. Would you consider dating him?"

"Don't much remember that guy."

"But, would you date him? I think he seems to say he has Communism beliefs."

"Oh please, you have to be kidding me. My Mother tells me stories about what she had to go through leaving Russia when the Communists took over that Country. No thank you, not for me."

Surprise. That very next day, Stanley quickened his steps toward me.

"Hey, Diana. Can I ask you a question?"

"If you like."

"Could I ask you for a date?"

"You mean me?"

"I do."

"I'm sorry, but I don't date men who aren't Christians."

There were no other words spoken. He went his way and I went my way. Apparently, he wasn't interested enough to know what that meant. I didn't want a future without God, I wasn't willing to walk down that road. God knew the man I needed to come courting. I just knew I wanted to follow the Lord.

Mostly every Sunday morning I would walk the mile from my house to the church on the hill. I liked the walk, whether it snowed or not, it was a pleasant enough walk. Sometimes, my neighbor, Jean Myers would come with me but not always. It wasn't unusual for a neighbor on the next block from us who would come out and talk with me.

"You need to come home with me, I can show you a good time."

"Oh, really."

"Yeah, anytime, just come to my house."

"Whatever." Of course, I never did nor did I ever intend to. It wouldn't have mattered what happened in my home but an invitation like that didn't sound like I wanted any part of it. I was in my teens and an older man can show me a good time? No thanks. However, anytime he saw me, he'd invite me over to his house "for a good time" but I continued to ignore it. I'd never discussed anything like this incident with my parents, I knew they would only come apart and probably call the cops on him and then I'd have to explain. I didn't want to have to face that. My life consisted of knowing when to keep your mouth shut.

Then I didn't understand. However, as I remember, I mentioned this encounter with my girlfriend's father who happened to be an elder in the church.

"That man is not up to any good. Whatever you do, don't ever go to his house."

"I didn't intend to. It sounded too strange to me."

This was now in the 50s, and the day came when I was voted to be the next Vice-President of the Youth Group at Capitol Hill Alliance Church. My parents didn't like it a bit, they didn't think it was a good thing for me to be tied down in a commitment and especially having to attend meetings in the evening. At the time, I hadn't really thought about it and I knew that I was being overprotected by my parents but I was willing to keep this commitment and I did.

Then this incident happened, I had a call from one of the Elders of the Church accusing me of Gossip in which I really didn't have any part. I was aware that my youngest brother and his friends had used me as a scape-goat but I wasn't about to accuse anyone.

"First of all, I know nothing about what you are saying but I think my response has to be that you must accept my resignation as Vice President of the Youth Group."

The elder insisted, "If you want to do that, you have to come and appear before the board. You can't just resign your position as Vice-President of the Youth Group. You can't just quit."

"Watch me. You have my resignation, I'm done."

I'm not sure the elder understood that he was talking to a 17-year-old. At that age, I didn't mess around. I had already approached the Pastor on one other occasion.

"Pastor, our youth teacher is telling us, that when we go to be with the Lord, that Satan will still tempt us to sin. If we do, we would be expelled, condemned just like Satan and sent to hell. This is just not what the Scripture says, you know that."

"I'm sorry, she happens to be a supporting member of the church, I can't say anything."

I was stunned. I was a teenager, not a member nor was my family. It was then I realized that unless my family was a supporting member of the church, what I reported as fact, was of no consequence, it just wouldn't matter.

As a result, when I was approached by the elder, enough was quite enough.

I hung the phone up, still looking at the phone in my hand and thinking to myself, *what do I do know, where will I go? What Church can I find?* I was truly afraid, I never intended to quit going to church and now I would have to find another one?

Not true to my eldest brother's character, he had overheard my conversation and immediately offered to have me join him with a new youth group he and his friends had just started in an abandoned chapel by the son of a local Pastor. I couldn't believe what I was hearing since he usually wasn't too thrilled having his baby sister tag along.

Elmer then said to me, "You'll never find anyone to come courting you there at Capitol Hill Alliance. Their youth group just isn't large enough.

Surprised at his statement, I accepted the invitation and didn't look back. It wasn't long after that, the same elder at Capitol Hill Alliance church called me once more and explained that I should come back because there had been a big change in leadership. I would be welcomed.

"I'm sorry, but I'm content to be where I am for now. I don't think I'm ready to come back."

From that time on, we attended the youth group that met in an empty abandoned chapel led by Ray Davies whose father was the Pastor of 45th Avenue Bible Church. We soon began attending that Church. It was a good group of youth, all with the same passion in following Jesus. We definitely learned scripture in a more practical way. Now we learned the practical side of the Scripture, where the rubber meets the road. I never regretted that.

It was at this church that I met Rev. Jack Hill from China Inland Missions and another fellow who was a Sales Person for Black and Decker products.

Pastor Rev. Davies was asked to minister to a man that had been incarcerated and was about to face the death penalty. Our pastor shared with us how God forgives all our sins. There is no sin that his blood does not cover. In that connotation, we still have to pay the price for what we have done, reaping the results of the sin committed. In other words, this young man that had taken the life of another, though he stood forgiven in the eyes of God, he would still have to pay the ultimate price. We reap what we sow and must suffer the consequences.

It was during this time, Rev. Davies preached the word and the Church increased in numbers phenomenally. The youth came from every direction to hear this man of God speak.

The church was led by the four elders of the church who would share in the preaching of God's Word. Membership consisted of believers adhering to attendance at the church, no official roll of members.

Our Pastor's father was a member of the "British-Israel-World Federation," who believed in *faith healing,* but to the degree of not accepting medical help for life threatening diseases. My parents, though they didn't attend the church, determined they would take me to see this man and have him pray for my healing from Asthma.

We did that, though I was surprised my Dad would submit to this but they wanted nothing more than for me to be healed. God did heal, that is for a few days. I asked my Pastor, "What do I do? I'm having difficulty breathing again."

He, in his wisdom to me? "Take what you need to take."

I did and then determined it couldn't be mind over matter. No matter how much I tried, I couldn't breathe without medication.

Mother at this time became very ill and none of us were wise enough to know why. Her Doctor prescribed medicine that had no effect for her. My brother Elmer suggested we call for "Davies Sr." to pray for mother. He came and prayed.

He said, "You understand, you cannot now accept medical help if you are asking God to heal you."

He left, but mother was getting very serious and we did have to call the paramedics. She was admitted to the hospital because she was bleeding to death. I was there at her bedside when the Doctor said, "Now, Mrs. Penner, you have had a long life and we can't promise anything. If the cancer has spread, then we'll do what we can."

They then gave her a hysterectomy, and she came out well.

Meantime, one of our elders was diagnosed with Lung Cancer. They prayed for him as well with the same message, "Do not accept medical help if you expect God to heal you."

The doctors made it very plain if he didn't accept the Medical wisdom of the day, he would have about six months to live. It was exactly six months and he went home to be with the Lord.

It was also during our time at this church that I determined to follow Jesus in baptism because I had turned 18. I had wanted to be baptized under Pastor Hauge's ministry but Mother was fiercely against it only because I had not yet turned 18.

She said, "You don't know what you're doing. You have to be 18 and then determine if you want to be baptized."

I wasn't really interested in arguing about baptism because I was deathly afraid of water anyhow. But this time I had made my decision to go through with it. Both my brother Elmer and I, then were baptized on June 16, 1956 at 45th Avenue Bible Church by Pastor Harold Davies.

It wasn't long after that, the youth in the church decided they would walk up Grouse Mountain, Following the path of the chair lift. I didn't know how I would do it but I did with a lot of wheezing and puffing. I made it all the way up but I'm sure the youth I was with would have preferred I wouldn't have tried to hike with them. They couldn't leave me behind, as a result it took much longer Though, I couldn't go down. By the time I had reached the top and with the increase in elevation, the air was too thin for me to move around at liberty. I did take the chairlift down with Pastor Davies.

Under the direction of the mature Christians of the church, we did *door to door* visitation. We were not to buttonhole people to attending the church but to make known our presence in the community and of course to invite them to come to the church.

Also, Rev. Jack Hill knew of my desire to follow my call to be a Missionary at the completion of my education. I had the unique privilege to also do *street ministry* under his supervision. It was through his ministry that I learned to view the circumstances and watch how God used him. Rev. Hill would say, "See the man just ahead of us? He is ready to accept Jesus." We would listen to this man, and then pray with the him for his Salvation. At other times, Rev. Hill would say, "This person needs encouragement, let's pray with him." I saw how God leads if we only are willing to listen for God to make the way very plain.

Then Bob, a Black and Decker salesman, would always say, "I am a Salesman and I have learned that when I want to sell a product, I have to stay on message. The message for the Christian is Salvation primarily. Let's not forget. People will always talk about excuses but our only message is that Jesus saves. John 3:16, stay with it. Then you have to learn to *seal the deal*. Yes, that's correct. If you don't *seal the deal,* you may have lost them forever to the Kingdom. Of course, unless, God in his mercy brings them in another way. We don't want to lose anyone from coming to know Jesus. It's the same principle I have to follow to sell my Black and Decker products. I have to make that deal, or I will have lost that sale and then I haven't made any money for my company or me.

Bob was also in a quartet and did a lot of singing with his group. He came by my place of employment on many occasions, but the last time I spoke with him, he expressed his inability to sing with his men in the quartet. He knew I had a severe Asthma problem, and that was when I learned he did as well. It was shortly after that, I heard he had suddenly succumbed to his condition. Apparently, the drugs his Doctor had given him for his Asthma caused his blood pressure to rise in excess and as a result he passed away.

This then became more of an urgent warning to me. It was in the back of my mind that I would seriously have to move to Southern California eventually. I knew once more how important that would be for me.

My brother Elmer was a very opinionated thinker and as a result, when things seemed to fall into *gray* areas, he wanted definite answers.

I asked him on one occasion, "There are no grey areas?"

"It's either right or it is wrong. No mystery. If you don't want to get yourself into trouble, just don't do anything wrong."

I thought to myself, *easy for you to say that. When does anyone not do something wrong? Life just doesn't add up that way.* Since this was his real concept in life, he tended to get miffed with the thinking of the elders in each of the churches he attended. He didn't always believe they were correct according to the Word of God.

As a result, he would leave to attend another church. This time he invited me to attend with him Fraserview Mennonite Brethren Church. My mother was thrilled since it was a Mennonite Brethren Pastor, C.N. Hiebert, who had married my parents in Winnipeg, Manitoba.

It was there I spotted a good-looking gal at his Church and told Elmer he should pursue her to be his future wife. He was serious about staying with the Mennonite Brethren Church while I preferred to stay with 45th Avenue Bible Church.

It had always been a dream of mine that I would eventually want to move to California since that was the place to live for someone with my illness. I had been saving my money diligently. My family was very aware of my desire, and when I turned seventeen, my mother suggested I apply for my birth certificate. I simply thought, why now? I did follow through on that advice. I paid the fee and soon the birth certificate came to me in the mail.

"That's not my name. They have the wrong person."
Mother said, "Let me see that." She showed it to Dad.
"My name isn't Dan, it has to be wrong."
Both my parents looked at one another as they examined my birth certificate.
"You know, Diana, because you aren't eighteen yet you can apply to have your name changed and it won't cost anything."

I didn't even have a middle name. I remember being disgusted. Both my parents knew all along, that there would be a problem that likely Dad had created. *No wonder Dad didn't ever call me Diana, and the name Leuene was fictious.* Should I have been surprised?

Then I remembered. My mother had often times told me that because their first two children died early in life, they couldn't give me as nice a name as Paulina. They would deceive Satan, fool him so he wouldn't find me.

So much for trusting God.

I did apply for a revised birth certificate.

Chapter **TEN**
The Preparation

By now we were all in our early twenties and soon most of my friends started leaving to attend Bible Schools of different choices. Some to Berean Bible College and others to Moody Bible Institute as well as Vancouver Bible Institute. I still wasn't sold on the idea of leaving my home and my job in a step of faith to attend Bible School. For me, it would be a huge step of faith because I would have no financial backing unless I worked for a living.

My memoirs are about **My Journey on the Road to Emmaus**, as God revealed Himself to me, bit by bit. Though I know the Scriptures say, God is not a respecter of persons, and He doesn't favor one over the other, I do feel favored of God. Then why wouldn't I, God always commends those who follow him as he promises to direct our every path. I like to think of it in that He was willing to protect the Children of Israel, in the same manner, he guides and protects his adopted children and loves them dearly, actually, enough to die for us. That's how I attempted to walk with Jesus on a daily basis.

It was at about this time, some of my friends had already started to attend Bible College in Alberta.

"Diana, you should consider Bible School, don't you think?"

"Peggy, do you realize the cost of attending Bible College? How could I ever save enough money for that?"

"We do gratis work at the school for tuition."

"You do what?"

"We work at the school. That helps pay for our tuition."

"Gratis? For real?"

"That's what I do."

"And after that, what will you do? How will you find a job?" Then what?"

"Trust God, something will happen."

"But that's just blind faith."

I think Peggy ignored that comment.

"Why don't you come to our Graduation Ceremonies. After the Ceremonies, the Bible College has a huge Conference. Come and see if you like it? Can't hurt."

"I don't know."

"Just do it. There will be a few of us going. We're going to go as a group. We're taking the train on a Family Plan promotion. The accommodations include bunk beds, eating in the dining car. Everything's included and it's not very expensive."

Peggy told me the cost and I accepted with much trepidation. After all, it was the first time I had ever left home. I condescended to go because I thought it might be a good thing to do, a weekend away from home.

My parents were quite open about how useless a Bible School Education would be.

"Going to Bible School is useless." Dad would say.

"You spend all your hard-earned money and when you get back home you have nothing."

They would say, "It will never get you a better job, nor make you more money. It couldn't better your status in society and even if you wanted to go into full-time ministry, you would have to find a paying job."

They didn't believe the offerings of a church could amply support a minister and his family. After all, they were witness to the fact there was never enough money to rear their own kids, how would they be able to help pay the salary of a pastor? They truly felt that a Pastor should never ask for money, he should do as others do, work for a living. Working in the Kingdom of God wasn't real work. After all, the important thing would be to get established in the workforce for the sake of financial security.

You didn't ever want to experience that lack of money. That was almost understandable. Hard times had hit my parents living through the Great Depression with a large family and then in the city. They had to live through those times with no money for medical help when needed. Those were the days when you went to the hospital in an emergency situation and no one was allowed to help until you laid the money on the table. You had to have the money to be attended to for an illness. Working hard wasn't enough. Thus, the discussion about how useless a Bible School Education would be for anyone.

I had no plans on the subject.

However, I had been saving for the possibility of obtaining a Green-Card to emigrate to the U.S. sometime in the future. Eventually, I wanted to move to California. With earnings of $150 a month, there wasn't much left for savings, but this was 1957. Still, I tried and did accomplish it. I had saved enough for that. It wasn't to pay for the green card, but that I wouldn't become destitute while in the US looking for work.

I was busy working on a career in Cost Accounting in a family owned business, a Pump Manufacturing Company. My brother Elmer was there as their machinist and Tool and Die maker. I decided not to continue on with my Education ambition. I had finished the eleventh grade. However, by this time my high school teachers had no respect for quality education, rather they began introducing the obscenities in literature as books to study. This was at the end of the school season, 1957.

With the fact that I came into public school at the age of nine and now I was already voting, I had quite enough of this craziness and the fact that I had already taken almost all of my last year classes anyhow, I decided to be a dropout and continue to work. Yes, I didn't have a high school diploma. Being who I am, I left school. I reasoned I'd never have enough money for college so instead, I chose to work for security in the workplace, for a future so that I shouldn't be left without a job in my working career.

Until one day, that family-owned company decided they needed to increase their profit margin. My boss actually discussed with me the thought of laying off the older staff in view of the fact that a younger person could come in, work harder for less money.

That was okay until I saw what that did to these people. I stood with these older people as they related to me what had happened. Just a few short years from retirement, and now with no income to see them through.

"What am I going to do? I invested all my money in this company. I believed in it."

I absolutely knew that God was showing me what that meant. There was no security in life outside of God. What was the point here? Where would the guarantees be? There were none outside of God's plan for my life.

I started to take life seriously. I began applying for work in other more reliable companies with better benefits, where the employees would be a part of a larger organization. Less chance of losing a position and possibly more of a chance to move upward in promotions. I started to apply for work everywhere, mostly so that I could experience how to present myself to different employers for employment. How could I convince them that I could do that job they had been advertising?

Then I suddenly awakened. I started smelling the coffee, realizing the four of us siblings were still living at home. Our parents had all four of us to give their attention to. Let me tell you, God knows how to lead.

It was now 1961, my brother Joe had finished his four-year stint with the Royal Canadian Navy. He had found a wife and was about to marry his bride, Judy and re-locate to the greater Seattle area. My eldest brother Elmer married Betty, a Mennonite Brethren gal (the one I had suggested for him), leaving home to start a new family in the Richmond area in Vancouver. Then, my youngest brother, Clarence, who had a hard time finding employment in our deprived economy at the time, joined the

Royal Canadian Airforce. He would be leaving for boot camp in days.

This was all within a one-year calendar period. That would leave me and my parents at home alone. I was terrified. I knew for certain my parents' attention would be wholly on me. I wouldn't be able to do anything without them medaling. Already, I was overprotected and constantly reminded of what I could and couldn't do because of my illness. I wasn't so sure I wanted to live with that.

Finally, the ideal job came up for me, I just needed to meet with Eaton's of Canada for my final appointment. This was it. I would continue to work in the office as a Cost Accounting Clerk. Most importantly, it would be with a very large organization in which I would have opportunity for promotions to advance my future. Also, my benefits would include discounts on what they sold in their Department Store. That meant, not only clothing but whatever I might need in the future. However, if I did accept that offer, I'd still be living at home.

At this point, God made it very clear that He was still calling me and I needed to seriously consider Bible College. I started making my inquiries. My parents were convinced that I could never afford it, so they didn't worry. Why would they? True, I didn't have enough money to make it to graduation but I could do it for one year. God knew that.

I'm certain my parents believed I was living in a dream world. They didn't worry too much about my leaving home. However, with the knowledge that Christian Colleges were allowing students to do gratis work for tuition, could I now squeeze a couple of extra years out of my budget?

Surprisingly, every school I researched was willing to allow for gratis work. I checked out Azusa, Canadian Bible College, Simpson Bible College, and a few more Christian Colleges.

"If you choose to go to Canadian Bible College in Saskatchewan, you will find out in a very short period of time, they will have to send you home. You will never survive the prairie climate. Be aware."

My Father said, "You know, that is one reason we moved from Winnipeg to Vancouver in the first place."

It was that comment, *sent home due to illness*. Those were the words that pulled me out of attending School at the age of 6. I remembered that. They probably were correct and I didn't want that.

I'm easy to get along with. I then suggested Simpson College in San Francisco, California.

My mother vehemently insisted, "You can't go there. That is a very evil city, a very dangerous place." They feared for my safety. "I do not want anything bad to happen to you. I'd have a heart attack if something happened to you there." It was, after all, 1961 when I made all my inquiries but I must say, I was oblivious as to what the U.S. was going through with all their racial problems. Not a clue.

My parents were aware, they also knew, for me, California could be a good choice health-wise.

My brother's wife Betty, a Mennonite Brethren gal, suggested I attend Fresno Pacific. Mother lit up with excitement. This was where the Pastor that had married my mother and father, in Winnipeg, Manitoba, was now living.

Reedley, California, the next town up from Fresno. She was excited that if I went to Fresno Pacific, she and Dad could renew their fellowship with that Pastor and his wife. Of course, as she said, there would be someone to look out for me. I wasn't really sure about that, but if that's how she thought, then okay. God works in mysterious ways. Sounded good to me, like I said, I'm easy to get along with.

There was one other problem since I had never graduated from High School. I know my parents were hoping against hope that I wouldn't be accepted in any College. Again, this would be one of my pipe dreams.

Mother said, "You know you have to be careful about what kind of work you ask for at the School. You can't do just anything. If you aren't careful and start to do housework for people for your tuition, you could very well end up with an Asthma attack. Dust won't do you any good. You need to think about that."

I knew only too well, she was right. Every weekend it would be my job at home to do the dusting in the house and every weekend I would be ill. I knew that without the reminder. So, what did that mean? I needed to specify what I could and couldn't do. I did that.

Surprise, I was accepted at Fresno Pacific and also, I would be doing my gratis by becoming the Dean's secretary. Turns out in the Canadian school system, I had earned more credit hours than I needed for College. Now, all I needed to do was wait for my emigration for my Green-Card. My appointment was set for the first week of September, 1961.

I had another problem. As it was, for me to make my appointment I would miss the first week of College. My fear of being late was so great that if I couldn't be on time for an appointment, I'd have to miss it. My fear was so extreme that I asked the College for an education visa instead. I had obtained that within a few days. Sounds foolish, but God knows what he is doing and isn't that awesome? We serve an amazing God.

I already knew what it was like as a child when illness caused me to miss school. Now, because of my fear of being late and missing out on the beginnings of the school year, but most of all, if I were to delay too long, I was very afraid that my parents would talk me out of my decision. There would always be another reason I shouldn't go and my Father already had a track record of making big plans, inviting multiple people over to our house and then quite suddenly, he would cancel the entire party. This had happened on multiple occasions. I wasn't leaving anything to chance.

Meanwhile, I heard rumors of how the Holy Spirit was very active at Capitol Hill Alliance Church. The information trickled down to me via my eldest brother that some of the neighborhood young men had responded to God's calling. Apparently, a battle was ragging with a few of the young men. The story goes like this:

"Please, Don, would you drive me to church? I'm late and can't get there on time walking."

"I have to wash my car."

"Please, I need you to do this for me." Fran ran back in the house for one more necessary item.

"Don, let's give her the hose."

She came out when she stepped into the hose full blast. Without another word Fran retreated into the house for a change of clothing.

"Let's go to her church and see if we can sit in her seat when she's dried out and gets there."

"Don and his friend left for church and sat in the center of the congregation. Minutes later Fran came in as the service had already started.

"Fran, come sit here."

She gingerly came in and sat down.

I'm told there were five young men that came to know the Lord during that Evangelistic Campaign over the two-week period.

I thought, *things are really happening at that church.*

_____

I decided I didn't have time anymore to seek out the land. I had a plan to somehow get a way to attend college and I was feverishly working on that plan. There were so many fears, but God was dispelling them one by one. Such as I needed a Christian College to be able to not only get a Bible School Diploma but I needed to cap off my secular education as well. Christian Colleges required students to attend a secular college at the same time as working on their religious education. Didn't sound easy to me. I'd have to find my way from school to school in unfamiliar surroundings.

Fresno Pacific it was. We were now on the road to California with my brother driving the car.

Surprise for me. I enrolled in Fresno Pacific College, and for my Bible education, I only had to walk across the campus for me to get to the Seminary. All our religious education was taught on Seminary level. In the end I earned my Associate of Arts Degree after two years of College and all the Bible I needed.

Meantime, because my health had proved to be good in California, my parents decided to proceed with plans to obtain their emigration to the States so that they could be near me. My Dad then discovered he wasn't born in Canada, but in the States, in Langdon-Cavalier North Dakota.

Canada had failed to find any reference of my Father's birth but he knew his parents had come into Manitoba from North Dakota. All those records had been lost in a fire of the records building. Now, he knew he was not a Canadian but how would he prove his American Citizenship? This in itself was a miracle of all miracles. He needed a witness that could testify they knew my Dad when and where he was born.

That person was found who knew both my Dad's parents. He signed the affidavit and within a month of signing the document, the man who signed the notarized document died.

My Father was now an American Citizen though he had voted in all the elections in Canada. God is always on time. This also meant my mother was not a Canadian after all. In the US she would have had to apply for citizenship which she had not done as of yet. That meant she was still a Russian Citizen and that she didn't like in the least.

US immigration had also told Dad that they would grant citizenship to all of his children. Each of us would only have to appear before them and sign the papers. This in itself should have been impossible because one of the clauses states that if a person has voted in their other country, having Citizenship in the U.S. would be forfeited. However, the U.S. immigration struck that clause out for my Father, myself and my siblings. We were instructed that our file would be kept for a 10-year period, we'd only have to come in to complete the paperwork.

Remember, I didn't go through with my emigration appointment? Now, because I missed that appointment, I could complete the work for my US citizenship instead of naturalization. I didn't need to apply for a Green-Card. I say, we certainly are special in God's eyes.

_____

Returning home after College and now working as a Cost Accounting Clerk for Canadian Kenworth, who's manufacture medium was heavy trucks. I became extremely ill. Bronchial Asthma had always been a disease I would once again be plagued with. Doctors were not always in agreement at how it should be treated. Some said it was caused by stress and could not kill anyone. Before I left for College one of my acquaintances passed away due to complications caused primarily by the disease. After returning from College a very close friend's dad passed away from that same disease, mostly because there wasn't a definite treatment. I was suffering at the same time.

My parents wanted to hospitalize me but were told there wasn't anything more they could do. I lay on the living room couch when the paramedics said, "Being in the hospital won't do her any good. Keep her home."

However, God wasn't done with me yet. I was told of a Christian doctor who had some success with treatment. This was the beginning of the use of Cortisone, the miracle drug, the cure-all. That did not come without complications.

But my call ... what about my call? My mentor, Jack Hill, from China Inland Missions, presented me with the possibility of going to Haiti. It had always been my goal only now I knew it wouldn't be possible. Here I was, physically I couldn't answer that call. I was waiting on God. That isn't always easy and God knows that. So many mistakes I could have made as I waited, yet God kept me.

I was engaged to be married to a Christian man, who, when he came under pressure, thought it okay to beat his girlfriend. We were seven weeks away from being married, and I knew this was not the path I needed to walk. There were other courtships that I couldn't take seriously because nothing seemed to mesh according to me. Finally, I decided I could take care of myself working for a living. It wasn't going to be so bad. If I had to make it on my own, maybe now I could.

After College, and now living in Burnaby, British Columbia, I became a member and attended Killarney Park Mennonite Brethren Church in Vancouver for about 5 years. I had a slight problem with the belief system and ethnic classification. There were also a few differences in Church Doctrine that I never did accept but with the Mennonite Brethren denomination, it didn't seem so important to them. At the time, their church constitution decisions were more about the do's and don'ts, what's good and what's bad for Christians in Society and not so much on Scripture.

That I would perceive because as an Ethnic group, they would feel that their people should already know the Scriptures, their families should have done the teaching. I need to say, none of the do's and don'ts was a problem for me anyhow. Keeping up appearances was what my family always had done anyhow. As I recall, that had always been the code of ethics in my family.

At this point, they certainly believed in good and proper living and of course the ten commandments. That wasn't the issue. It began to appear to the youth that the elders in the church were living a hypocritical life. When they were in America, alcohol wasn't accepted but when they traveled abroad, and since it was accepted in other societies, it would be the right thing to do.

However, it soon became a more predominant issue, for when at social functions, many church members would do social drinking. Finally, the denomination decided it would now be acceptable stateside and everywhere else.

Even at that, none of this was my issue. In the late 60s in the Mennonite Brethren Church, unmarried women would sit on one side of the church and the young men on the other. Married couples and families sat in the middle. If you were an outsider or just didn't pay any attention and came in with a friend and sat in the center, the gossip would flow. For me, since I didn't sit down and learn all these cultural necessities and I might say, I wasn't reared in the denomination, it soon became time for a change of churches. It was always assumed a person was born into the culture and therefore there was no excuse for not knowing the rules and customs in that Church, after all, my roots were supposedly from the denomination.

However, I had been taught so well by my Pastor at Capitol Hill Alliance Church during my teenage and early twenties, I was convinced that the Scriptures would have to be my guide, not rules and regulations of the Church. The rules were already beginning to change in society and soon a lot of the rules wouldn't be followed anyhow. It seemed to me, Capitol Hill Alliance was still teaching the scriptures only instead of the "do's and don'ts of society.

Mostly the part I missed was with The Alliance it had always been about all people, it didn't matter the color, the language or financial status, the ethnic background or where people were from. I asked the Mennonites at a church youth function when they would be willing to reach out beyond themselves. They said, "It's coming, but give us time." To their credit, they did have one such couple at the time, not of their ethnic group. I soon tired of the running along ethnic lines and issues.

I was now working for Robert Morse and getting very restless. I knew I needed to do something and a vacation in Hawaii looked good to me. Would I have to do this alone? I hooked up with the Narramore Christian Foundation group to avoid going alone. We landed in Hawaii June 1969, the same day as the US landed on the moon. Walking into the Motel, we sat and watched on TV, the astronauts walking on the moon.

Came home to find my Dad was in the hospital with Lung Cancer. On August 28, 1969, one day before his 69th birthday he passed away.

All in all, it ended up a total of ten years from the time I left for college including my stint with the Mennonite Brethren Church and my teaching American Chinese students at the Vancouver Rescue Mission Sunday School.

I had already moved into an apartment that would allow Mother to move in with me. The Lord began nudging me. *Are you saying, Lord, I should go back to Capitol Hill Alliance?* To me, it seemed it was the right thing to do and now the right time.

It didn't take long before I was busy in the church leading a youth choir and at the same time doing a bit of solo singing. My mother would also attend the church with me. As it happened, Rev. Peter Wittenberg, missionary to Germany, was now Pastoring our local Church which made my mother very happy. She felt that at last, a Pastor could understand her. She tried to share with him a hint of her life in Russia but never more. He seemed to accept her for who she was.

I convinced my mother that she should join the church along with me. She needed a church to be concerned for her as she was getting older.

By this time, I already knew most of the youth from prior years that were attending the church. We were all still single and we knew, even though Pastor Wittenberg wanted us to join with the younger youth, that wasn't about to happen. The time seemed right to organize an older group and so we did. Our only stipulation was that every one of us had to be single, including anyone we invited to have our devotional time.

As a result, we invited a young single pastor who had returned from ministering in Saskatchewan. He had been there about ten years pastoring churches.

"Diana, you must already know Bert."

I said, "I do?"

"You both worked at Canadian Kenworth at the same time."

"Possibly, I didn't much mess around with the guys in the shop. I knew you, Alf, were working there."

"Anyhow this is Bert." We were introduced.

"Hey, how would you like to be our Devotional Speaker on Friday?"

Bert said, "I'd love to."

He accepted. The plans were made.

"Are you still working at Kenworth?"

"No, I work at the boys' ranch in Haney, with Pastor Wittenberg."

After that particular Sunday evening service, I joined my mother to drive home. My mother proceeded to say, "There goes my future son-in-law." I said, "Impossible, with the last name like Linn? Not going to happen." She didn't say anything more.

Our Young Adult group was about to meet at our regular meeting time. However, at the last minute, everyone bailed on us except for the four of us. Three women and Bert.

"Sorry, Bert. But, guys, why don't we scrap the devotional and go for dinner in China Town. Okay with you Bert?"

"Okay with me."

Unknown to me, Bert didn't much appreciate Chinese food at the time. But to make humorous conversation I had Bert write on my chopsticks for a momentum, the time of our dinner occasion which he dated on the chopsticks (I still have them). In God's economy, Bert invited me for coffee after dinner.

The first thing Bert did was ask me, "Have you ever been married before?"

"No."

"Do you have a Bible School Education?"

I do. I graduated from Fresno Pacific with an Associate of Arts degree and enough Bible. A Mennonite Brethren College."

I was taken by surprise. Impressed but surprised. Actually stunned. I couldn't believe I was hearing this. Was he courting me? Apparently, I had all the right answers.

"Bert, tell me about your education and how long have you been a Christian?"

"1962, I was saved during a two-week crusade by an Evangelist, Dr. Malyon from Moody Bible Institute. I went directly to Canadian Bible College for a year and the following academic year it was less expensive to transfer to Briercrest Bible College so I did. Almost immediately the District Superintendent sent me to Parry Alliance Church in Saskatchewan. At the same time, I pastored a very small church near there in Saskatchewan as well. They were very good to me at that church.

After that I asked to transfer from the comfort of a wonderful caring church that had been so meaningful for my ministry to something with a bigger challenge. I was sent to Wawota Alliance Church, a church plant that was just starting a building program. I helped to get them through to their dedication and then I left. That's when I came through an 80 degree below zero snow blizzard to drive to Vancouver."

"You live at home?"

"I do."

"Well, I guess I do as well.

"Right now, I'm commitment to Timberline Ranch in Haney, B.C. and Rev. Peter Wittenberg for one year of Alliance Ministry."

"Almost 10 years, right? That is since you came to know the Lord?"

"It is."

In my mind, I should have heard, "Bingo," but it just didn't yet register.

From there, it was out for coffee every night for the next 47 years, only now it is iced tea. The rest is history.

I remember Bert would come back from his work at the Boy's Ranch in Haney after 10 at night and give me a call to go for coffee. I would accept the invitation, have coffee (caffeinated), visit together, come home after 11 at night and couldn't sleep for 4 hours because the caffeine had kicked in, (no, I knew it would, there really was no excuse). I'd Get up for work the next morning at Robert Morse. Could be that's how I learned to live with less sleep. It worked, or I should say, I went to work with very little sleep, but my love for Bert was growing yet my energy level was waning.

We did a lot of hiking in those days with our young adult group. We hiked up Diamond Head and another of our group, a missionary lady in training, asked Bert many questions. I listened to Bert's answers and at that moment when I saw how he responded to the needs of needy people. I said, *this is the man, if ever I should marry.* I knew the gal in Missionary training was also looking to interest Bert. Then I said, *what will be, will be.*

Chapter **ELEVEN**
Meeting My Fiancé's Family

Vancouver, British Columbia in 1971. Prime Minister Pierre Trudeau married Margaret Joan Kemper, a Canadian author, actress and social advocate. Developers were about to develop land in front of the world-famous Stanley Park. On May 29, 1971, about 70 hippies took matters into their own hands. They ripped down a fence and stormed onto the site to plant some maple trees, then set up camp in tents and ramshackle huts. They called it All Seasons Park, and their squat lasted for almost a year.[6]

In August of that year, a Gas town Riot ensued. A few months later, September 18, 1971, Bert proposed, and of course, I said yes but I had a very important question for him now,

"Do you object to moving South of the Border, into the U.S."

"No problem with me."

From there we introduced each other to our parents and told them of our plans to marry. They seemed happy for us, but

---

[6] The Vancouver Sun

interjected and asked Bert about another lady he had previously been introduced to by his family, I presume. I never pursued that, thinking Bert asked me, what do I care about the someone else.

Bert's Mother said, "You two should get married before the end of the year. That's a big tax advantage, you know. We have our basement you could live in until you find a Church. You know, Bert, your brother did that when he first was married."

My gut churned into knots. *I don't even know these people. I've never lived with other people before and besides, I thought I was marrying Bert*. We were both already in our early '30s and stuck in our ways. We'd have to learn to blend those ways together. I wasn't ready for another adjustment. I would have to have a serious discussion with Bert. That would be the impossible mile.

A December wedding for us? I was still working and hadn't planned to leave just yet. The wedding needed to be on my Vacation. That would give me time to plan. It had to be February and I would have preferred the 14th but it didn't fall on a Saturday, so we chose the 5th, the first day of my planned vacation. I get a bit practical at times.

"Don't worry, Diana. We are not marrying my parents, nor your Mother. It is going to be just you and I. This will make the adjustments just a little easier. However, I do have one concern and that is my mother. What if she has a heart attack? Should we postpone it then?"

"My opinion is, we can never really know how our parent's health will be when the day comes. If we postpone for the *what if's*, we'll never know when or for sure. I say, no. Let's just do it and let God take care of your and my mother."

Then quite suddenly, my mother started to put up defenses. I couldn't quite understand. It seems my eldest brother had decided that I should not marry and leave my mother because he felt it was my responsibility to take care of her.

However, I knew that God had called me, and for certain the Scriptures say, *"Follow me, and let the dead bury their own dead."* Matthew 8:22; *"everyone who has left houses or brothers or sisters or father or mother … for my sake …"* I didn't really care about the reward but I knew I had to follow and leave the results up to God. And yes, I was sad for Mother but I knew God would take care of her and her needs.

In the end, unfortunately, my eldest brother didn't continue on to serve as a missionary candidate, although he faithfully served the Lord in the churches he attended and led boy's groups successfully, for the glory of God. He was also involved in Street Ministries extensively.

Here's where I learned to type 120 words a minute, not at first but eventually. This was the time of manual typewriters, not self-spell checking. That's right, it wasn't because I was a speed typist, it was out of sheer necessity. For lack of an office, Bert brought his manual typewriter to Confederation Park. We sat on one of the outdoor tables and I typed. We needed a place to serve, a church to call us.

"You want me to do what?"

"We need to send our resume to churches and see what God has for us."

"But I'm not that good a typist. I've been working in Cost Accounting, not in secretarial jobs, I've never worked as a secretary."

"Believe me, Diana, I can only use one finger to type. You'll do better than that."

This was now the beginning of the rest of our lives. We pulled the prayer manual with the list of Churches. With my health situation, we knew the west coast had already proven itself as being acceptable. Outside of that, there were no available churches to serve in Vancouver. Certainly, in our eyes that might have been our choice.

Here we were, ready to apply in churches south of the border. We stood at the post box, letters in hand, prayed that God would be in total control, that He alone would lead us to where we needed to be and then we dropped them in the mailbox.

One by one, the letters came back with no availabilities. Rev. Dyer from California did answer but said if we were to come to California, the only position available would need a Pastor that would be willing to have a part-time job in secular work to subsidies the ministry. It was where I really wanted to be but we would have to pray about that one. If we did that, likely I would be the one working in a secular job. Though my desire was to be in California, we would have to go into prayer and see what God wanted. It had to be his will, not ours.

Chapter **TWELVE**
Joyce Bible Church
Our First Church Together

We were sitting in the kitchen of my future in-law's house when the phone rang. It was a call for Bert from Rev. R. Rogers Irwin.

With the phone in hand, Bert asked, "Diana, our District Superintendent is calling to ask us to serve at Joyce Bible Church, in Washington State. Do you want to do this?"

"Love to."

Here's a Historical critique of Joyce, Washington ... founded around 1913 by Joseph M. Joyce. The town of Joyce is located on the State Scenic Highway 112, 16 miles west of Port Angeles and 33 miles east of Clallam Bay. The town of Joyce has a historic general store originally opened in 1911. It has a museum, cafe, and other business establishments.

When we arrived in Joyce, at the time we were there, it was impossible to see any kind of settlement because, as we always said, there is a home behind every tree (that is, at least 200 of them) in 1971.

The arrangements were made. We drove to Joyce, Washington to candidate. Now (this many years later) it is comical. We were given directions to drive down Highway 112, "you'll go through two large dips in the road. When you do, turn left on the next road after that. My house is the first house on the left. We'll be waiting for you." That was the directions from Wilson Myers, the elder of the church.

The appointment time was set. We drove to Port Angeles and because their mailing address is Port Angeles our assumption was, for this particular board member, he would live in Port Angeles, right? People don't always live close to the church, we knew that. By the time we arrived in Port Angeles, we couldn't imagine how we would get to those dips in the road. At the edge of town, we saw a few homes, we decided to knock on one of those doors to inquire. Surely, his place would be nearby.

"Wilson Myers? We know him. He owns the Machine shop in town. I work for him. No, he doesn't live in town, he lives west 17 miles from town. You have to cross the one-way bridge and then you'll come across the 'dips' in the road."

And so, we continued on over the one-way bridge along highway 112. Remember, this is before cell-phones. Finally, we came across the little log building, a church called, Joyce Bible Church. By then, we knew we had missed the dips in the road. We knew that at least this had to be the Church. There was a small Post Office, a restaurant almost next door. I'm sure Bert made a phone call from the restaurant to the board member apologizing for the lateness of the hour. After being reprimanded, Wilson Myers arrived at the church so that we could follow him out to his house.

I should have mentioned that I had never lived beyond the big city of Vancouver. My entire life was in the city. My first four years of life were in the City of Winnipeg and the rest in Vancouver. My stint in Fresno, though not a city as large, had 100,000 people at the time, but nonetheless was still in the City. Did people really live just off the side of the highway? Who knew? Apparently, not me.

Nothing had prepared me for any of this. We were in the interview process when, Wilson Myers said, "We were thinking that you and Diana could probably live in the parsonage we showed you earlier."

Now I hadn't been with them to see the old parsonage but Bert had told me about it. I thought to myself, Bert had described the building as half of it being sunk into the ground, leaving the floors mostly uneven. All I could think, Oh, please Lord, you know I wouldn't be able to deal with this. As this was presented to us, I sat there and wondered what Bert's response would be. I knew full well I would be living in a damp house in an extremely wet climate.

"I'm sorry, but that wouldn't work for us," was Bert's response.

I was never prouder of my future husband than this time. God really knew what I could and couldn't do and now I was convinced my fiancé understood.

Another of the committee proceeded to say, "You won't have to. The church has already purchased a Modular home for the new parsonage. It should be delivered and on the property by the time you are both married and come back from your honeymoon."

Okay, Wilson Myers comment must have been a just in case situation. After much deliberation with the board, we accepted the call.

"We will definitely accept the call to this church to become your pastor. You must take into account that I have to get my Green Card and I know that can take a while. We are willing to come out on weekends.

We anticipated a long wait for Bert's immigration papers. In the meantime, we would be traveling for Sunday Services every weekend until we could get everything completed.

"Would the wait be amenable to the Church?"

"We are certainly willing to wait. We will give you whatever documentation you could need to get this completed as quickly as possible."

We were young, early 30s. It would be a challenge to make the trek but we were up for it. The only complication was the many miles we would be driving every weekend. The choice would be crossing the water onto the Peninsula or drive around via Olympia, Washington.

Every weekend we chose to take the Ferry onto the Peninsula and then drive to Port Angeles taking the 112 over the one-way bridge.

Meanwhile, we went through the immigration process, completing my Citizenship, which I had been informed was waiting for me any time I was ready.

Bert began his paperwork and as I may have mentioned earlier, I had a whole roster of paperwork already completed for my appointment and then didn't follow through. Bert was able to use copies of everything I had, so when we stood at the wicket in the immigration office, they said to Bert, "You will need ..."

Bert said, "Is this what you want? Here it is."

Each piece of paper they requested Bert handed to them. The Immigration Officer asked, "How'd you do that?"

From there it took a total of seven weeks to completion and Bert had his blue-card in hand. Apparently, I'm guessing for clergy it was slightly different (but I don't know) but this was at the end of 1971.

That Christmas must have been the most memorable Christmas I had ever experienced. It snowed for the December weekend when we were invited to attend Joyce Bible Church for the pre-Christmas festivities. We would be driving to the Church from Vancouver. This was December 1971.

"Are you taking your car?" My Mother asked.

"We are. It has fewer miles."

"You need to put your snow tires on."

"I don't have much time."

"It won't take long. Just go now, you'll have it done before Bert gets here."

I had studded snow tires, I wasn't worried about the weather. I couldn't take any chances with the car when I had to drive. It was done and back in short order, and on time.

It was a beautiful snow scene, with the fluffy snow still on the tall fir trees. Everywhere we gazed, white with freshly fallen snow. Pure, white as snow, always reminds me of Isaiah 1:18, *"though your sins be as scarlet, they shall be as white as snow; though they be red like crimson, they shall be as wool."*

Bert had his Blue-Card which meant he could begin to Pastor the Church starting January 1, 1972. He would come down to visit me every weekend until our wedding day.

It was February 5, 1972, in Capitol Hill Alliance Church, a beautiful sunny day, with only a spattering of snow still on the ground when we married with Rev. Peter Wittenberg officiating at our wedding.

Everything that could go wrong went wrong or so I perceived it. A friend had volunteered to take care of handling the food, that I would provide. A week before the wedding she called to say she wouldn't be able to come.

Unfortunately, we couldn't afford a Wedding Photographer. Needless to say, we have no *in focus* wedding pictures.

To keep everything to continue on in the *going wrong part*, at the wedding, my vail wouldn't stay in place. It didn't end there, though.

We had a long lecture from our Pastor who insisted I should find someone to give me away, usually customary for the bride (at least in Vancouver, B.C., apparently). I felt we were too old for that. I insisted that historically it had been done before, and we would be both walking down the aisle together.

Bert drove our car down the hill to park in the parking lot of North Burnaby High School, next to Confederation Park. The high school was both our Alma-Mater. Another car came by him, not two feet in front of our car without stopping at the stop sign.

"What are you doing, man? You almost hit me!"

The driver was about to approach his car, "I'm sorry, I'm sorry, Sir. My brakes failed."

"I can't talk now. I have to park my car and hurry to the church. I'm getting married at 2 o'clock and it's 1:30 right now." Bert ran back uphill all the way to the church.

I walked up the stairs, standing at the front entrance of the church.

"It's almost 2 o'clock. Does anyone know where Bert is?
I said, "He'll be here."

"I don't see him anywhere."

Then someone said, "There he is. He's coming up the stairs."
He made it right on the minute, 2 pm, ready for us to walk down the aisle together.

At that very moment, one of our elders of the Church came to Bert to tell him his mother was in the study and could be having a heart incident. This had been one of our greatest fears, that either my mother or his would have a heart attack.

Bert went into the Pastor's study then and spoke with her for a few minutes. He came out and we were able to continue.

We had a very special blessing, in that our pianist and vocalist, was a couple planning a future in music and had volunteered to play and sing for our wedding.

With the music playing, it was now time to walk down the aisle. As we proceeded to walk down the aisle, Bert's brother blurted out, "Bert it's not too late to back out now." I do think he had too much alcohol in his system at the time, or the family was still opposed to our marriage? I did remember that they had chosen a Scottish lady for him but I had supposed that she wasn't to be my fiancé's choice. I never debated that.

The reception was held in the basement of our church. It had been mother's dream to have at least a sit-down light dinner for our guests. The ladies of our church rescued the reception and took care of everything for us.
Our M.C., Jack Hill, from China Inland Missions, led the reception for us. After all the toasts were finished, Bert said, "We will be back to say goodbye to each of you and Diana will throw her bouquet for you. She will be wearing her going away outfit at that time."

We left in uncle Bert's car, (Bert's mother's brother, his name sake). I remembered it to be a red convertible.

"Diana, you will get changed at my Uncle Bert's house and then we will begin our journey on our honeymoon." I didn't know anything about these arrangements.

"Don't I have to go back and throw the bouquet? Won't they be waiting for us?"

"I arranged for Jack to have them sing a few hymns and songs to give us a head start out of the country. They won't be following us."

"Well if that works for you, it certainly works for me."

We drove away, I changed and we left for the border. Our honeymoon had begun and we never returned to the church.

Joyce Bible Church gave Bert his Salary in advance and told him to leave for our Honeymoon. We drove to Bellingham, Washington for our wedding night. From there we spent our Honeymoon in San Francisco for a week.

Arriving in San Francisco, we parked the car in the Hotel lot, walked over to pay Motel 6 for the night. No wallet.

"What do we do now, Bert?"

"See if we can find it. Hopefully, you dropped it in the car."

Bert had given it to me to hold. I held it all right but then forgetting I had it, while getting out of the car, dropped it. We walked back to the car and there it was, beside the car in the parking lot. Remember, this is San Francisco. God certainly does take care of us. Now he's learned, never give me something to hold, I'll forget I have it and let it drop.

Our honeymoon was eventful as we rode the cable cars to tour San Francisco and enjoyed the scenes of Fisherman's Warf.

We arrived back from our honeymoon and were given a small 8' mobile home to live in. This was to be a temporary situation. The Modular Home was to be delivered soon. However, the city had a problem with the drainage of the land on which it was to be set on.

So here we were, after much scrubbing and cleaning we settled in nicely. Though it was a tiny home, but then there was only the two of us. We stored our wedding gifts in the attic of the church. In my mind, I bemoaned the fact that I couldn't use any of our wedding gifts, but I needed to keep that in check. There was the promise from the church eventually this would all change for the better.

I might just want to refer back to my earlier years in High School, Home Economics cooking class, as I recall, each student was given a gas oven to prepare a meal. We had to prepare dinner with the idea to learn how to have a complete dinner ready precisely all at the same time. However, as I said, we had to use a gas stove. I would light my oven and put my meal in it. That is, I lit the match and assumed it was lit. Our teacher was a very wise teacher. When she could smell the gas odor, she first opened all the windows in the classroom and you guessed, it was my oven that had the gas coming out, not burning.

All this to tell you why I hate gas stoves. Our tiny trailer had a gas oven. I already knew I would have a problem so I made Bert aware. I was sure I had lit the gas but wanted him to check it. Somehow, my fear of fire causes me to pull the match out too soon.

Bert came to my rescue and lit another match and proceeded to light the oven. It gave off a tremendous explosion, with a burst of fire and shot us both out through the closed door of the trailer. Bert's eyebrows and the front of his hair was singed. This was a Monday evening and as I recall the men had a prayer meeting Monday night that he had to attend. This was the first hair cut Bert insisted I had to give him out of necessity. He didn't want anyone to know our dilemma.

"Diana, you need to trim my hair."

"I've never cut a man's hair before."

"You have to do it. I have to be at Church in less than an hour and I can't go like this. You have to do it."

I proceeded to do it and I must say, that time at least, it was a good job. He left for the men's prayer meeting and no one was the wiser. Needless to say, I insisted on pulling some of our wedding gifts so I could use my electrical appliances instead. It is no wonder why.

During the time we spent in that trailer, on one particularly cold night our electricity went off. I couldn't figure why all the neighbors in the trailer court seemed to have electricity. Bert insisted they might have battery operated lights.

When the morning came, we still didn't have electricity. You guessed it, some of the youth in the church pulled the breakers. We turned them back on but never spoke of it to anyone.

A couple of weeks later, after the morning service, we were told we needed to clean up the trailer and move to a Motel at the edge of town.

"We don't have time. We have to move out, like right now and I have a service tonight." Bert felt consumed. They were asking too much.

"I'm just going to tell them to forget it. That's just too much."

"It's okay Bert. We'll do it."

We worked feverishly and were able to accomplish the job. God enabled Bert to preach the evening service. God was truly in control. Indeed, He was our enabler.

That move took us to Indian Valley Motel for a few more weeks as we continued the wait for the Modular home to arrive on the Church property. It also would be where we would entertain the missionary for our first annual Missionary Conference, as a couple.

Now reality set in. I was married to a pastor, came to a new country (sure it was my birthright), a new church, a new job. Shock waves rolled over me. Adjustments had to be made for both of us after all, we were both really familiar with our own habits by now (did I say we were both 32 and soon we would have a birthday coming up?) but I have the most wonderful husband anyone could have. He stood by me and helped me as we both adjusted. We made our changes as time progressed.

My Journey on the Road to Emmaus — Diana E. Linn

Before I married Bert, my mother warned me that being a pastor's wife was no simple plight. She would know me better than I knew myself and she knew how seriously I tended to take life.

An elder of Joyce Bible Church came and said, "Pastor, Mr. Wetherell passed away last week. We were waiting for you to come off your honeymoon so that you could arrange the service."

That was the very first day we arrived back off our honeymoon, the first ministry responsibility for us. This wasn't that big of a thing for Bert, as he had already served a combined 10 years in Parry and Wawota, Saskatchewan. He was already very familiar with these ministries, only I wasn't. Even so, who enjoys ministering in times like these, in sorrows such as this? I just didn't know how I would handle funerals but Bert insisted I really didn't have to say anything. The important thing was to be there for the family.

"They don't want advice. They want the comfort of having us by their side."

However, God is amazing. He certainly knew very well my personality and he was about to teach me to feel with the bereaved but rejoice with the joys of a wedding that very week. Bert had the privilege to marry a very dear couple, Merton and Debbie Corey. Merton, a prominent Church member had just recently finished his service with the military in Viet Nam and was soon to be a Bush Pilot with MAF. This was truly a time of rejoicing.

An interesting 'side-bar' connected with their wedding in JBC, our first wedding at JBC. Bert told me, "I remember Mert Corey saying 'if you guys try any shenanigans with me or my Bride tonight' ... as he pulled out his revolver from his suit vest. Further stating ... 'You guys will be doing the barn dance Polka in the parking lot of JBC ... Remember that.'"

Foundation

Modular Home in Waiting

While we served In Joyce Bible Church, for our entire ministry there, every time we had a funeral, that very week without fail, Bert would marry a couple. You have to believe how precious our God is, He really does know us.

Some people came because they wanted to be married in a church that had been made of logs and some merely because the bride's name was Joyce. Then, of course, people from the Church as well as from the neighborhood came.

_____

There has always been a premise that whatever is donated to a church must be kept there for eternity. After all, it must have been ordained of God and if nothing else, it must be kept in remembrance of the donor family (at least at Joyce Bible Church). However, this principle would not hold in our ministry. In our ministry, parishioners must be sure their donation isn't just a hand-me-down that they felt guilty about discarding. As a result, they felt compelled to donate it to the Church. The better part of wisdom would be to donate it to someone who can repurpose it, but never to the church. The church is not a house of storage, rather a house of prayer.

After some discussion with some of the church people, it was decided that Bert and Merton Corey would start a huge fire. Oh, did I say fire? I did. As the old sacred pews, with gas poured all over them, flames burst up. They were consumed in a hurry. The fire Marshall arrived to see what this was all about. Then did I say we were only yards away from the Olympic National Forest? By the time the Fire Department arrived, the fire had nearly been reduced to ashes. The Fire Marshall left satisfied.

There is an important principle and lesson here. New Pastors in the ministry (this is supposed to be the humorous side of us), do what you have to do the first year of your ministry, you will be forgiven. If you wait, don't try what we did.

However, the fire did its job and the pews were no longer. From there it was clean up, dress up, bring the Church back to its original beauty.

Once we were situated in the new parsonage, it wasn't unusual to have deer come to see us at our sliding back doors. Our puppy would bark from the inside enticing the deer to come see what was going on.

We made a practice of one major thing while in Joyce. Taking time off to be with ourselves at least one day a week. There was a men's meeting every Monday and Bert had to be present. As a result, there was no Monday off for the Pastor. We would choose another day but this was in the early days when gas cost 27 cents a gallon. We could afford to take a day and drive to Olympia, 120 miles out for a day off. It was not uncommon to be overcast in Joyce when the Sun couldn't break through the clouds for days.

In Olympia the sky would be clear, the sun shining brilliantly. Then to walk through the Malls in Tacoma where there were people. Especially around the holidays, to see the decorations. For me, this was my relief valve, my break into reality.

While in Joyce, Washington, on our days off, on our way to Olympia, we would often deviate our driving and go through Shelton, called "Christmas Town USA." As it happened, we usually drove through on very raining cold days.
Everything looked so dreary, and to me, that means nothing but sadness.

Shelton is at the bottom of the rain forest, (an average rainfall of 60 inches per year) so the rain was to be expected. We'd drive past Shelton Alliance church and I'd say, "Oh please, Lord, not here, you wouldn't call us here. It's always so dreary."

Bert would agree with me, "I don't like it either."

That's probably not what you should tell God. Or, could it be that God was saying, "Remember this place. You might not like it now, but you will when I call you."

Then there were the times we would drive up to the Heart-O-The-Hills, up in the Mountains of Port Angeles, Washington, 16 miles from Joyce. We'd find a campsite, pitch a tent. We had all the amenities of camp life we could afford. For us we did the unwise thing, we used our propane stove to make our food in the tent. We were careful and were fine. I'd advise against this vehemently. It is just not wise, especially if you are asthmatic, like maybe me.

Joyce Bible Church proved to be a very loving caring people for our entire service time with them. Church was held in the Old Log Building that had been made with the timbers on their land and milled by the people of the church with their own private sawmill.

The Church was exceptional.
When we arrived off of our honeymoon, Wilson said, "Here is a key for a locker in town. Bert knows all about it."

"Thanks, I will give it to him."

A key for a locker in town that Bert knows all about.

That is what I intended to do. But to me, it has to be for church paperwork, I'll give it to him later, he's busy with Church people right now. That's how I had it figured. In my previous job, I would deliver paperwork for our company often. That makes sense. At this point, as I said earlier, it would be important to know that I was not only born in the big city of Winnipeg, Manitoba but then I spent my life growing up in the big city of Vancouver. Even the years I spent in Fresno, California at College was in the city of Fresno. I worked in industry, bought all my food from Grocery stores. My working career was all about cost accounting and paperwork in business. Often, at Galbraith & Sully, my boss would frequently ask me to run a batch of paperwork for Microfilming and storage to another company uptown.

Okay, here I am with a key in my purse. I knew I would need to give it to Bert as soon as it was appropriate, supposing that would be when we got home that evening. Remember, we were in the throes of getting situated from one living place to another as well as from one culture to another. First in an 8 Foot Trailer and then to the Motel, so in the course of activity, I totally forgot.

Therein lies another problem I have. Give me something to keep, I will proceed to put it in my purse for safekeeping but never remember to deal with it or that I even have it.

I might tell a story as a young child. As a kid, when we were living in Vancouver, my father had a store in town that he sold small decorative furniture he had made. Every evening after work we would open the store for business. This one particular evening my brothers were playing with the keys for the store. I was so annoyed that they might lose the keys. I finally snatched the keys and hid them. As it was, my brothers lost interest and we all forgot about it. Well, you know where the story goes. After we had dinner and it became time to leave the house to go to the store, my dad couldn't find the keys. We all searched the house everywhere and couldn't find them. Then when it was too late to do anything about it, I remembered. I hid them between the back spokes of one of our wooden chairs.

This wouldn't be so funny except that we were about to have our annual Missionary Conference at Joyce Bible Church and we would be entertaining the missionary. I looked at Bert and said, "What am I to cook? We don't have anything for me to make." He agreed that we could at least cook up some wieners and potatoes, at least have something. He insisted, "The Missionary will understand."

The missionary arrived, when I suddenly remembered I had a key to give to Bert. "It's for a locker in town. Wilson Myers gave it to me to give to you."

Bert blurted out, "That, Diana, is a locker full of meat, in case you are wondering."

"And how would I know that? I wouldn't know anything about that. I thought it was papers for the church you were going to need."

Bert, I and with the Missionary drove to town in an effort to retrieve some of the meat from the locker. Everything was labeled nicely. However, I didn't know what the abbreviations meant and neither did Bert or the Missionary.

"Okay, Bert. This must be Ham. That's what it says, right?"

"It does."

I prepared for ham but found out it meant hamburger meat. How should I have known the key was for a locker in town with a side of beef?

"Okay, we can do that, then."

I might add, we had many very good missionary conferences at that Church. Joyce Bible Church was a non-denominational Church but affiliated with the Christian and Missionary Alliance. They liked to hire Alliance Pastors which enabled us be on loan to them. As a rule, they supported many Missionaries as well as those from The Alliance. They preferred to give to our Missionaries personally. For certain, it was greatly appreciated by each of the Missionaries that were sent to JBC.

The parishioners were keen on learning at the feet of God. We also learned much from these loving, caring people. Some of them came to know Jesus through our ministry for which we are eternally grateful and some of them we only learned about when we returned to Joyce Bible Church in Joyce, Washington, to celebrate their 20th Anniversary.

We were invited to take part in this Anniversary Celebration. To us it seemed to make sense that we would be driving up to Joyce for the afternoon service, why not preach at

Shelton Alliance Church? Bert preached and then right after the church service, we drove up to Joyce Bible Church to join in the Celebration. The problem was it is 114 miles of driving through the twisting and turning of the highway. It took slightly longer than we had anticipated reaching the church by the 2 pm hour. We made it, a little late, but we made it. We quickly jumped out of the car, leaving the windows down for Mitzy, our toy poodle. Hurried into the church. The service had just started

One of the Elders introduced Bert, "We knew Bert Linn has arrived, by the barking of the dog."

Nonetheless, they asked us to stay and Bert to preach that Sunday night as well. Why not? What else could possibly go wrong?

When I grew up in the Church in my younger years in the Alliance, I was convinced women went with the styles of the day and wore their Sunday best. We felt it showed reverence in God's house, but also, we had to keep up appearances. That still works for me to a degree. I was shocked when people came to the church in jeans. The women tried to convince me that even I could wear slacks to church.

However, I am who I am. I can change with the people and culture of the time, but I guess you'll always see me for who I am. Even in Joyce, the men would come in from hunting to lead the singing in the Church and the type of clothes were not so important. God chose to use them just as they were.

As we moved from pastorate to pastorate down the coast going south from State to State, the dress code changed. The farther south we were and now into the 2018-19, as I write my memoirs, often, the pastors don't dress in suits and ties unless it happens to be a funeral or a wedding. I still try to keep up appearances and attempt to look my best. Times change and change is always good.

Often, we like to debate the issue of change, maybe it's because we don't want to comply. It's easier or so we think, to stay with the status quo. I will say, the farther south we go, it is more like the wild west. I used to think that meant, only along the west coast. No such luck, it includes Arizona even more so.

I do think that with my generation, being that the hippy phenonium came just after us, it did affect how I thought. The sixties brought tremendous change to our cultures. It seems from that time on, change was happening and if those that were leading the way ahead in the Status Quo and didn't catch that scene, they would forever be somewhat unaccepting of our modes. Though the Gospel never changes, yet the mode must for the way we are, not the way we were.

There were a few spotlights while ministering at Joyce Bible Church. A couple from the community had come to have their marriage performed by Bert and in our little log cabin Church. The fellow was a muscular logger with his petite bride. When they came for counseling the groom insisted that it was to be a very personal wedding with just his witnesses, parents and themselves. So, it was to be about five to seven people in attendance at the most. His bride was aware of the groom's wishes but her parents wanted just a little more for their daughter. Apparently, the bride didn't inform the groom of her mother's desires and the plans began to formulate.

On the day of the wedding, the groom arrived, awaiting his bride and for the wedding to begin. He was in the backroom with my husband as he listened to Bert's encouragement while they waited for his bride to arrive. We were aware that the church was filling up, but he was not. It was their wedding and they needed to have their wishes fulfilled, that is, the mother of the bride's requests, not his.

The groom looked through the glass window that connected the fellowship hall to the church. Suddenly he saw people kept coming into the church. His face turned ghostly white, as he realized there were more than just a few people in attendance. He was still okay, or at least he was still standing on his own two feet. The church continued to fill up and if fact, it was beginning to be overflowing with guests. Even the balcony, that hadn't been used in years, began to fill up.

The bride arrived and Pastor Bert along with the groom proceeded to the front of the church, to await the wedding march. Since it was to be a small wedding the wedding party had failed to arrange for music to accompany the ceremony. Foreseeing that some piano playing could be a necessity, Bert had convinced one of our ladies, Linda Newton, to play just a few songs, it wouldn't be much. The pianist informed us that she could only play two songs and one of them was not the wedding march, that was it. Pastor Bert told her that should be enough. It was better than no pianist and she was the only one available.

Finally, the couple was together at the front of the church, both standing before Pastor Bert. However, just as Bert began the words for the wedding, the groom fainted. Bert motioned to the pianist to continue playing. She could only repeat those two songs. The groom was assisted up and seemed to stand just fine. Pastor Bert started again, he fainted again. Bert motioned once more to Linda that she should continue playing the piano. She started again with those two songs. A third time, the groom fainted. Finally, Bert asked for a folding chair for the groom (not for his petite Bride, but for the burley logger, the groom. The groom sat while his bride stood beside him. After Bert pronounced them man and wife, the groom and the bride proceeded down the aisle but with the wisdom of Pastor Bert, he summoned two elders to walk with the groom until they would reach the outside of the Church.

Just before they reached the double doors, the groom began to slump but the elders held onto him tightly, one on each side until he was outdoors. He made it but it was an ordeal for him.

One wonderful blessing we had while at Joyce Bible Church, the loggers in the Church were also hunters and fishermen. They would bring us buckets of smelts and sockeye salmon, all the fish we could eat. I mean fresh. I've never tasted any fish as good as we would be given there. Because they were also hunters, it meant they would bring us venison. I learned to clean fish and cook wild meat. They also brought us a side of beef each year. Now they gave the key to Bert instead of me ... a learning curve for all of us.

I realize that I'm the type of person that can get bored very easily, and since I was not employed outside of the home, (at least for now) became the self-declared Pastor's secretary. Now I would have to seriously learn how to stay on budget. As a result, making food from scratch became fun. I chose to make most of our clothes. However, I never gardened. I did know it was expected of me but I'm not into the mud thing and my excuse is my allergies. That's a big deal for me. I did tailor my husband's suits and all my clothing from knitting to everything we needed. Almost everything except for our shoes. Well, almost everything.

In the Pacific Northwest District, it seemed that District Conference would always be held at Canby Grove Camp. This was never my favorite to have to live in the trees and weeds at the campsite. That was good and well until my allergies would kick in. Yet, in spite of saying that, we spent days off camping in the Heart-O-the-Hills in the Olympic National Park on a regular basis. There must have been different weeds there, none that I was allergic to.

At District Conferences, I also learned how to knit sweaters in one easy step. The two sides of a sweater at one time and on one needle and the two sleeves at the same time on the same needle. Awesome work with good results.

I also devised a ministry report card to realize the trend in God's leading in the church, which proved invaluable for us.

───────────

God had performed a miracle in my life and healed me during those years in that church. Scripture says if we are ill, call for the elders in the church and have them pray. We did that. Then God revealed to me that on a particular day my healing would be complete. I told Bert and we marked it on the calendar. I'm a total believer that when God heals, I will know because no longer will I have to take asthma medicine. I will no longer need it. I'm not a habitual pill taker, I only take what I need when I need it. Not always what the Doctor says to do, and often I pay the price for that thinking. This time I knew I simply wouldn't be needing it. I don't believe my miracle was to be mind-over-matter. Divine healing is God's choice for us to glorify himself. If it pleases him, it is always for our benefit as well. I don't have to try to be well. When He heals, I am well. I have no doubt in what God wants to do.

The day came, and I remember it well. I said, "Bert, I don't seem to need the breathing medicine anymore." We both looked at the calendar and sure enough to the day, God's promise was fulfilled. God does care for us.

We tested our faith to be sure God had performed that miracle. We went to the farthest northwest corner of Washington State, Cape Flattery. It is in Clallam County, Washington on the Olympic Peninsula, where the Strait of Juan de Fuca joins the Pacific Ocean. It is also part of the Makah Reservation and is the northern boundary of the Fuca Pillar at Cape Flattery, the northwest extremity of the Olympic Peninsula.[7]

We walked down the steep cliff to the water. That wasn't enough, we walked back uphill to where our car was parked. I had never felt so good. God does take care of his people. I know we are special to him. I quickly learned that God could never be put

---

[7] Wikipedia

into a box, He would always do what would glorify Himself with us in the ministry. We learned that at Neah Bay, 17 miles west of Joyce, Washington.

Sometime later we were sitting in our living room and looking through our Yearbooks from high school. I looked at Bert's group graduation picture.

"Well, I can't believe this. You're that guy!"

"What guy?"

"You're that guy. Your picture, Bert with the crew cut!"

Remember I told God about my requirements? That's right. Bert Linn had the crew cut when I met him and had already spent ten years as a pastor. Does God answer prayer? It was then that I shared with him whom I had asked God for.

As I was preparing to leave for College, Bert was one of the four men who had come to know Jesus at Capitol Hill Alliance in the two-week Crusade with the Evangelist, Dr. Earnest Malyon, from Moody Bible Institute. It was there that God met him and called him into the ministry.

For about four years plus we had now been serving God in this church, God began to show us that He wanted us to move on to another field of ministry, another careworn church. He said, *"put your affairs in order, I'm working on your call."* I'll bet your wondering where that could be.

My Journey on the Road to Emmaus   Diana E. Linn

Chapter THIRTEEN
So, Send I You
Shelton Alliance Church

    The time had come for us to follow God's lead once again. He was calling and our District Superintendent had informed us that we could candidate at Wolf Creek Alliance Church in Oregon. It is a very beautiful location with serious people following the Lord, and they needed a Pastor. They had two preaching points, we would have to serve two Churches at this place. We were certainly not opposed to that.

    We arrived at the Church and on Sunday Morning, Bert preached at the main church and then immediately after drove a few miles out to the new church plant.

    Some of the people at Wolf Creek Alliance Church, said, "Let's go hear Pastor Bert at the other Church. See if he is the same there as he was here."

They did that but Bert happened to overhear their plan. He and the Lord decided it would be a different message at the other location.

One of them reported back, "He didn't preach the same message."

It was a great experience at both of the churches. Then, after all that, there was a 3 to 4-hour interview with us after the services. It went well but neither of us felt convinced that this was our next call. We knew there could quite easily be a call to the Church plant, but hesitated about Wolf Creek Alliance Church. We proceeded to District Conference at Canby Grove Camp.

Rev. R. Roger Irwin approached us, "Would you like to Candidate at Shelton Alliance Church? I've already heard from Wolf Creek and they and you weren't convinced."

Bert and I looked at one another, I said, "We'd love to go to Shelton."

Before we drove back to Joyce, Bert preached the morning service and decided if God wanted him to become the new pastor at this location, then he would give an altar call and there would have to be a response. This was his fleece, but if no one responded, God wasn't calling. Someone did respond and as a result, the church called us.

Looking back, God chose us to unravel the situation in each of these churches but at the same time to comfort the believers so that they could grow and move on. It's not the stars that we could accumulate in the ministry but rather a call to go where few would dare to go. What a privilege to heed God's call. It is where he wanted us to be and we knew that very well. God was leading again.

Shelton is a primarily industrial city on southwest Puget Sound and the seat of Mason County. It consists of a 6.11 square-mile city. Since its founding, Shelton's history has been intertwined with that of the logging and lumbering industry, on which the town's economic well-being continues to depend. The town is named for David Shelton (1812-1897), who served as a delegate to the territorial legislature, which was originally known as Sheltonville.[8]

God does know what he is doing and that's exactly how it happened. He called us to Shelton, Washington and to Shelton Alliance Church. When he gave us that call, we knew it very well, it was now the only place we wanted to be, even though we both agreed over and over again, saying if Shelton Alliance Church is the last Alliance Church in the District, we still wouldn't go there.

Strange, but to us, it was a breath of fresh air. This church was through and through Alliance, Alliance to the Core.

This was the end of 1976, and they were very endearing, a Four-Fold Gospel believing Church. A Church after our own hearts. They were famous for saying, if they called a meeting then there would be an offering.

Gayle Callanan was our very talented teacher who worked in the public-school system in special education with special needs children. She became our Education director.

Needless to say, we had an exciting children's ministry in this church.
A Multi-Media program, with 15 Minute Stations for children to learn the lesson being taught for the day. As they moved from

---

[8] **HistoryLink.org**

station to station, they would teach the same lesson, only 3 different ways. There would be a lesson, maybe a flannel graph for 15 minutes then a TV type that had a film strip for them to watch. After that, the fourth station would be reviewing the memory verse. With this system, it wouldn't matter if some students were mentally challenged or gifted. The 15-minute span was easy for the teacher and the student. It proved to be an amazing concept.

The District became aware of our method of teaching and brought other Alliance Churches to learn how we were accomplishing this achievement.

It soon became evident to the Church Board the church needed a Youth Pastor. Denny Tyas was called and became Bert's Assistant Youth Pastor. It was shortly after Dennis started his ministry at Shelton Alliance Church that he was able to study and became an ordained minister. Denny eventually married Gayle Callanan and together became Alliance missionaries in South East Asia for years.

I will never forget, with Bert's innovative techniques in the creation of Robbie Robot, a device made up of scrap metal with a shoot that would accept money for missions. It was devised to welcome the collecting of only pennies for missions from our children's vacation Bible School. The excitement buzzed through the neighborhood with the local banks complaining that we were depleting them of all their pennies. Bert said, "Just wait, you'll get them all back at the end of the week."

Bert performed many weddings and some were outdoors in the State Park. One in particular ceremony, we were all hoping the rain would hold off just long enough for the ceremony but it didn't. Back in the days, I would type up the entire Wedding Vows, especially done for the Bride and Groom. We had one prepared that was all nice and neat, that we intended to give to the bride knowing rain was very likely. However, the bride insisted she wanted the one smeared with the rain. She wanted to remember how it all happened on their special day. "Okay ... here you are."

During our stint in Shelton Alliance Church, my husband's father was in his last days. We often drove up to see him on the long drive to Vancouver, B.C. but while in the hospital, my mother-in-law invited Bert in to see his father at which time his father came to know Jesus as his personal Savior. Soon after the passing of Bert's Father, his mother was adamant that she wanted to visit our Church in Shelton. She came to the service and gave her life to the Lord as well. That indeed was a blessing the Lord afforded us.

Usually, in the Churches we served, seldom would we be afforded medical coverage. God always provided us with Doctors that would charge the clergy less so that we could afford what we needed in spite of the lack of insurance. Then, we began having dental issues. It was then I chose to supplement our income by finding a job.

First, I attempted to work with Head Start but soon realized, I was not equipped to work with children from troubled homes. I needed to work where my gifted skills would take me.

It soon became evident that we needed to fulfill our own obligations. This was also because I frequently had the need for medical care we couldn't otherwise afford. Obviously, the feeling came with a certain amount of urgency for us.

Work came quickly and I began working in Banks instead of manufacturing. As a result, I had to learn a whole new industry and became a loan clerk. I appreciated the practicality of the money side of life. Learning lessons from how people handle personal finances easily taught me how not to fall into money traps. Good lessons on how not to abuse money. but instead making it work for you (not that we ever abused money).

In those days, God enabled us to do much. I could work all week, keep the house clean and ready it for classes to meet on Sunday in our home and be beside my husband in the ministry. Let me tell you, I was younger at that time. From that point on I worked in secular work as well as in the ministry with my husband and I still would always be his secretary.

Notoriously, after getting the much-needed promotion in a short amount of time at Capitol Savings & Loan in Olympia, God called us to follow Him once again to a new field of ministry. That was never a problem for me if God was calling, I wanted to be willing to go. At this time in the working place, businesses were able to limit their vested retirement plan for the employees they hired. Capitol Savings & Loan had a policy that made it necessary for an employee to have a minimum of 10 years with the organization before they could keep the retirement plan, they had earned. We were able to see the plan and what the company had put into it toward our retirement. Of course, as a Pastor's wife, the likeliness that I would be in one place for ten years at this time was zero to none.

Soon, I was promoted to supervisor of the loan department with a huge raise increase when we were called to another ministry. We knew God was in control of what He was doing for us. We followed in obedience.

We resigned our ministry at Shelton Alliance Church along with Rev. Dennis & Gayle Tyas. The Tyas's went on to prepare for Missionary Service in the Dalat School for Missionary Children in Singapore, of course, a part of The Alliance.

Next, we were called to Roseburg Alliance Church. We decided to take one month's vacation or sabbatical before we started our service as Pastor there. It was approaching fall weather so we decided to take a road trip down the I-5 hooking up with I-10, driving across through Texas and to Florida. From there we drove up through Syracuse, Upper New York and then on through Buffalo.

We decided to take a tour Bus to see Niagara Falls on the Canadian side. It meant we would go into Canada for a few hours and then back to the U.S. Of course, we went through the Stores and I spotted a collection of Silver Spoons with each Province engraved. I just couldn't leave them behind but we hadn't been in Canada long enough for them to be Duty-Free knowing we would be re-entering Canada to continue on our Road Trip across Canada. We'd be driving all the way to Vancouver, B.C. which meant we would, in the end, have spent a goodly amount of time in Canada.

I did realize, that I really might have to pay duty, but thought it couldn't be too much. We boarded the bus, sitting and waiting for immigration officers to release the bus to continue back to the U.S. They asked everyone for their citizenship. At that time, in the late 70s, we still didn't need to show a Passport between Canada and the U.S. Then it was my turn to be questioned.

The immigration officer asked me, "Where do you live?"

"Shelton, Washington."

"Your citizenship?" He continued to ask.

"U.S. and Canada."

"You can't be both. Now, what is it?"

"Sir, I have both."

He insisted, "You can't have both. You either are an American or a Canadian."

I reached in my purse and pulled out my Document and showed it to him, It said Special Services. I might add, the U.S. immigration had issued the document because I insisted that we would often travel in and out of Canada, I needed something to prove my American Citizenship. Thus, the document, Special Services.

The Immigration Officer said, "Get out of here. Just go." He left and never did get to ask me about what I had bought to declare.

I said, "Thank you, Lord."

We completed our Road Trip across Canada and realized that we probably would never repeat that vacation again. At least not the stretch from Ontario through Saskatchewan, we felt there really was nothing to see but the flat prairies.

It was at this time we visited Wawota Alliance Church as well as Parry Alliance Church which Bert pastored before we were married, simply to renew our fellowship. I hadn't had an Asthma attack until we were about to drive and visit Bert's Seminary at

Briercrest Bible College campus in Saskatchewan. Not having an episode in years, I wasn't prepared. The wheezing was heavy and continuous.

As a result, we just kept on driving. It wasn't too long before we started seeing the rolling hills of Alberta.

Then into the Canadian Rockies. By this time, I was well again. Amazing! Now I knew I could be weather conditioned. Coming to the end of each of our ministries, we would be walking along and there would be flowers in bloom, trees spitting their seeds into the wind. Then I'd always have an asthma attack, ending up in the emergency for an injection to open my airways. My hands would shake and I'd have to drink through a straw because I couldn't hold the cup steady in my hands. After that and probably back into our house, I would be fine once we hit the Rocky Mountains.

My Journey on the Road to Emmaus   Diana E. Linn

Chapter **FOURTEEN**
Roseburg, Oregon

As we moved farther south, when Christmas time came, we brought with us the traditions from our previous church so that they could enjoy the benefits of what we had learned and enjoyed from our other experiences. One such event was chopping down our own Christmas trees from the mountains. It was here that every Christmas season the church would acquire tags from the Bureau of Land Management to go into the mountains to cut Christmas trees that had been tagged, for the church and other members of the congregation.

"My car can't go up into the high country in the snow." We had a 1979 Green Chev Sedan. Prior to that, we had a Red Vega that totally died on us while living in Shelton. Thus, the green car.

"Oh, sure you can." The men insisted we must come along. I made a large pot of Chili for everyone to enjoy and whatever else we needed.

We did drive up into the snow. Like Bert had said, "I'm stuck."

"That's not a problem, we'll get you out."

The men enjoyed pulling our car out from the snow. We brought down all the trees we needed for the Church and the people. The scenery and the experience was absolutely beautiful.

It was at this church we met the local Chimney Sweep couple, Stan and Holly Turnidge. They had left a profitable business income in California to come to the small town of Roseburg Oregon, trying to scrape up a business. We hired them to clean our chimney and to get the cobwebs off our basement ceiling that had been left in the Parsonage basement, assumedly for more than just a few years.

During our ministry, both Holly and Stan came to know the Lord as their Savior. We've retained our friendship with that family now for decades.

It was difficult to get into the work environment in Roseburg. Somehow, they had a philosophy not to hire people newly located in town. I waited and this is when God opened a door in a Credit Union. Apparently, some of the employees tried to do a strike on the organization. Since they were non-union, the manager decided to fire them, and that's when I was hired in a part-time capacity. As a result, I would work with Credit Unions for the rest of my working career. Their philosophy of business lent very well into Christian principles and ethics.

At this Church, we (that is Bert) had the outstanding privilege to perform a wedding for a Cartoonist. It was good to experience humor with people you ministered to. I'm very sure that my husband and I will never forget this one. Somehow, being very busy as always, and now have gotten to know this fabulous couple, Bert agreed to marry the couple on their given evening.

Everything went well until he came to the saying, "in front of all these friends and enemies..." instead of the customary, "friends and relatives." The church roared in laughter. Bert immediately corrected the verbal error and went on. It was a very good wedding in the end and I believe that couple is still married.

When we first came to serve at this church, many of the people shared with us the desire to move to a more visible and suitable location. Thus, the first step for us was to change the name of the church from Hucrest Alliance Church to Roseburg Alliance Church. A major feat in working towards a move was all the hard work with the major players of the Church who built the Parsonage as well as the building in that original location. No one wants to see their handiwork left behind.

We would have sports events that were bent around Potluck dinners with the people. Our biblical sermon *Talk Back Ministries* proved to be very profitable. The morning service Bert would share God's message about a biblical couple in the Bible and then in the evening, a family would be chosen to research that biblical couple to share with the congregation. Then we did a *Talk Back* in the evening service. This did two things. it allowed the people to understand the scriptures better and allowed us to see where and what the thoughts of the people were biblically.

It was also the Church of Potluck dinners. Is this the reason why I no longer care for Potluck dinners? They were good and a blessing but …

Once again, the Lord let us see just a glimpse to let us know we should be prepared for a move. It was now time. This had to be one of the harder times we had to experience as we had to take very seriously Psalm 27: 13-14, *"Yet I am confident I will see the Lord's goodness while I am here in the land of the living. Wait patiently for the Lord. Be brave and courageous. Yes, wait patiently for the Lord."*

We served there for six and a half years when God called us away. This time to Southern California and undenounced to us, a completely different ministry.

Chapter **FIFTEEN**
Following the Call into Rescue Missions

There were several liberal Churches in the area that wanted us to come and minister, but the leading was not there. God chose to have us wait on His leading. When the Lord wants to do an *about turn* in our lives, we very often have to wait on him to show us exactly what it is He wants us to do.

While we waited, some wonderful people wanted to have us live rent free on their farm in Sutherland, Oregon, just a few miles away from the church. Sounds wonderful right? We couldn't have asked for anything better than a free house to live in. Here's where I should've stepped back and let Bert and the owners check everything out. How would I know and why wouldn't I have to see where we could live?

We checked out the property and found the house to be in disarray. Actually, the sheep and wild animals had come to inhabit the house. I had forgotten that I had a tendency for Asthma attacks, I just hadn't had any for years, God had healed me. (Now that's another story: Maybe my next book. Who knows but God)? I should have known better, but why would I? You guessed it. The Asthma came back in a vengeance. Now I was so sensitized that I had to have strong medicine to get through these times. Pneumonia would now be my threat.

Meanwhile, Bert had a few handyman jobs, and with my part-time work at the Roseburg Credit Union, we continued to plow through and eke out a living. We purchased a Trailer Home that someone had just bought and didn't need anymore. It was still under warranty and a good buy that we couldn't pass up. At least we didn't have to pay rent but only for space to park it.

Soon we were called to candidate at Bly, Oregon. Sounded like a wonderful place to pastor. The people we stayed with were very accommodating but, had wool blankets on their bed, a cuckoo clock that wouldn't stop sounding every fifteen minutes. After a sleepless night and one in which I could no longer stop sneezing, nevertheless we went to Church that Sunday. Bert preached but like I said, I couldn't stop sneezing. The people we stayed with offered to have me see a horse Doctor to see if he could help me. We didn't go see that Doctor. Did they call us? ... I don't think so.

It was about this time in our Roseburg, Oregon transitions that we began thinking about more education, as we had to *sit out* for almost 18 months waiting on God for His next move for us.

In the past, R. Rogers Irwin, our former District Superintendent had suggested many times, "Bert, you need to beef up your education." While we're waiting, I suggested, "Maybe this is the time to be thinking about furthering your education. It's been years from when Rev. R. Rogers Irwin mentioned it might be something you could be interested in."

"I don't know how we would afford that, and not only that, I haven't been in a class room environment in years. How will I ever be able to do this?"

"Somehow, someway, maybe?"

Then I said, "Or, maybe rescue mission work. What about that?"

"I don't think I want to do that either."

In the meantime, Bert came across a Moody Magazine where they were offering a new program for Pastors who were already in the ministry but would be able to come for classes for a week and then go home and do the class work, taking only one or two classes at a time.

"I don't think we can afford that, either."

"Why not check it out. Maybe, you can do something to earn your way."

Surprise, surprise, Bert called and they offered him a scholarship. We just had to fly there, stay at the school and go to classes.

Now here came the journey to Moody Bible Institute. We flew via Alaska Airlines from the Long Beach Airport, or at that time called Daugherty Field. As time went on, we would fly from John Wayne Airport, directly to O'Hara Airport in Chicago, Illinois. Then we took the airport shuttle to LaSalle Street.

"There it is Bert, just like their picture."

Bert asked the bus driver, "Is that Moody Bible Institute?"

"It is."

"Can you let us off here?"

We must have looked like country dorks but the driver didn't hesitate to stop for us to disembark. We learned later the bus never stops in front of the School.

Moody's policy was to have the Pastor's wives audit the classes when possible and I did that for the most part.

The education journey began. It was in the time of manual typewriters and with Bert's one finger typing, I would do that part for him. We managed to get his papers prepared for each of his classes.

God had erased all his fears in learning and was able to come up with a 4.0-point grade average. The only glitch in the system was, that he would have to get his BA to make the MA official. Was that a problem for my husband?

It meant that he would have to take his BA from Briercrest Bible College in Saskatchewan, where he had already attended Seminary. The blessing was because he was a graduate from that school, he would not have to be on campus to earn his BA in ministry. He was accepted and now came the work while working on his Master's Degree at Moody. If it could be done, my husband was the man. By the year 2000, he had done both degrees those degrees as well his Doctorate from Northwest Graduate School in Seattle.

Following the call. That meant, God was calling again, in the midst of the education endeavor, Bert applied through Inter-Christo, a Christian Job availability all over the nation.

It listed the Salvation Army as an option. I asked Bert once again, "How about that?"

"I just don't feel led."

There were also opportunities with Village Missions. Bert said, "I just don't feel led to do deputation work. I just don't want to do that."

"I guess I don't blame you for that. That's always a lot of work to make the needs known and then you have to ask for money."

"I just won't ask for money."

It was now 1984. Finally, a call came from Long Beach Rescue Mission in Long Beach, California. Rev. Wayne Turley asked, "I want you to come and preach at the Mission. We'll show you around and then see if you like it. You would become our Senior Chaplain."

Bert said, "Well, okay, we'll come."

"This next weekend?"

"Okay."

As I remember, Bert said to me, "This is not the type of ministry I want, but we'll go. Preach but that's about it. I need to be obedient to the Lord, so I'll preach but that sums up my involvement."

There was a holiday involved and I would be off for the Thursday, have to work on Friday. I asked if I could have the Friday off at the Credit Union so that I could go with Bert. Somehow, the people in authority wouldn't give me the extra day off.

We went anyhow. It just meant I'd have to be back at work Monday morning. "We can do it. They want us both there, you and I, Diana. It's a job for the two of us."

We did it. Drove the 810 miles, taking 12 hours and 10 minutes after I had finished work for the day, arriving Saturday evening. Stayed at the guest house at the mission.

The first thing the Turley's did was to have us get acquainted with the facilities and the how's and why's of the Mission. Wayne Turley didn't even ask Bert to preach in Chapel (as was originally planned). Bert said, "If you heard me preach, why would you ask us to come." In response, Turley said, "Because, I know The Alliance."

Chapter **SIXTEEN**
The Long Beach Rescue Mission

"I'm impressed. This is not a normal mission. Everything is first class, clean and comfortable. The homeless get to stay in upper-class accommodations."

Apparently, the founder, Wayne and Jan Turley were also pleased with Bert's qualification with The Alliance and after a short meeting on that Sunday, while we were still there, Rev. Turley gave us a call.

"I want you to start right away."

I looked at Bert, "I have to give at least a 2-week notice. I can't just quit." but they wanted us as soon as possible. Two weeks was the soonest I could go. Two weeks it was. We would head home, driving most of the night. I took a shower and headed to work. Tired, but God was my enabler.

That Monday morning, I tendered my resignation, when the acting manager said, "We thought if we let you have an extra day you would end up leaving us."

"That's how God leads, in spite of us. Not because of us."

Bert said, "Here we go again ... once again, on loan from The Alliance to fulfill God's call in California. Now, in faith, "on your mark ... get ready ... go.

While at the Mission, Bert came in contact with Rev. Joel Comiskey, the founder of Hope Alliance Church. They were both at Kinkos making copies. Bert for his graduate studies at Moody and Joel for Hope Alliance Church.

Bert tells the story, "Running off a Bulletin?"

"Yeah, this is for Hope Alliance Church. I'm the Pastor."

"I'm Bert Linn, Senior Chaplain at Long Beach Rescue Mission."

Joel said, "I've been looking for you. You need to come to visit my Church. It's in my home."

We did, but soon discovered that the people visiting his church were also some of the people coming to the Mission or at least with the same set of problems.

"We only have a very few Sundays off Joel and I don't think that will work."

We spent the few Sundays we had at Long Beach Alliance Church on Sunday evenings, actually, the same Church Rev. Joel Comiskey attended.

We definitely had a very fruitful ministry at the Long Beach Rescue Mission. We were informed after we gave our resignation that we had more people that gave their lives to God for salvation and rededications than they had ever experienced. That truly was God, not us.

    Then the day came, as was usual for us, it seemed the Lord was beginning to reveal to us that something was blowing in the wind.
    "Bert somehow I have this strong feeling that the Lord is saying, "put your house in order."
    "I have that same feeling. God must be calling us into something. Let's just be obedient and do just that."
    And so, we did. We started organizing and throwing away stuff we didn't want anymore and generally preparing for some kind of move without knowing the direction. It had not yet been made plain to us.
    Meanwhile, the days at the Mission continued to be filled with emergencies. We would expect that. Shortly after that, as I was fulfilling my duties at Lydia House for Women, when one of the overnight guests or homeless women, came to me with a request.
    "Please, would you pray with me. Satan is torturing me, I can see him doing that to me. Can you pray with me that he will leave me alone? Please, so that I can have victory over him?"
    My very soul shuttered to think I should be praying in this case. I did.
    We stood and prayed together, believing that God would do just as she had requested. After we prayed together, the lady's continence changed. She was at peace. She thanked me and left to return to her assigned room.
    However, now it seemed Satan was about to attack once more, full force, but this time it was me he would attack. I was

called in the office at the Long Beach Rescue Mission and told I had no business praying with anyone for anything. That was not my job. I sat there in shock but I had no rebuttal, I just listened.

    God is certainly greater than anyone and His leading for us very evident. We already knew He was once more beginning to lead us on. On to where I didn't know. God knew. We had finished our four-year stint, at least mine was finished in my mind, I didn't have to ask anymore, I knew that quite well, so I tendered my resignation.

    I came home to tell Bert what I had done.

    "Guess what, Bert. I gave them my resignation today."

    "Surprise so did I."

    That very day, we got a call from our Pastor at Long Beach Alliance who invited us to do a Church Plant in Fountain Valley, California. God is always on time.

    At the same time, we were also offered and invited to accept the call for Hope Alliance Church. I said, "Bert, please, I don't want to do that. How can I deal with that anymore? Haven't we had enough of that type of ministry?"

    "I don't want that either. Let's just do the Church plant."

    It was at this time I put out my resume to a few Credit Unions for a job. It wasn't long before I had three job offers. I accepted the first one that came in but hadn't started as of yet. Then one came in that suited me much better knowing I needed the best job for us as we continued in the Ministry. As a result, I decline the first and accepted the second. After I had already started at Long Beach Schools Credit Union, I was offered another but then I knew for certain, I was already in the best place.

Then came the blessing. I had to attend a Credit Union training session with other Credit Unions.

Suddenly someone approached me, "I know you. You prayed for me at the Mission when I was there."

It was like coming home, an answer to prayer and God was saying, the Mission was, after all, a very worthwhile ministry.

"You are working with …"

"I'm a loan officer now with my Credit Union."

And so, we exchanged greetings. What a blessing God preserves for his own. For me, this answer to prayer was the catalyst for going where God wanted us. I'm really sure God always makes His way for our lives very plain. He makes the way straight. We don't have to wonder. It seems God uses methods right where we are.

I marvel at how God leads. He knew what we didn't want and He knew what He wanted to do for us. We continued on with Fountain of Life Church, a Church of the Christian and Missionary Alliance. We developed a wonderful music team and made some very close friends.

We did a blitz mail out and door to door invitations. We would share the church with the people and ask them about Jesus. Cindy and I came to another house and now it would be my turn to invite the people. I did that but was restrained by the Spirit. I could only invite the family as they shared their interest in the Church plant.

Going to witness together with another lady in our church, was a bit miffed with my approach. "You didn't follow the plan."

"I guess I didn't. That's just not how God led me this time."

From that time on, this entire family started attending the church and our outreach broadened. God was leading because he wanted that whole family and he was about to use us.

Keeping the story short, the husband came to know Jesus through Bert's consistent ministry. Then the brother was dying of cancer and also accept the Lord. It was at this point that their soon to be son-in-law also came to know the Lord as well. Bert had the privilege of marrying him and his bride, Kenny and Ruth's daughter.

When we listen to what the Holy Spirit has to say about our situation, then He can lead as He wills. When God led us to Arizona, that family soon after sold their house and joined us in Tucson. They re-located to Avra Valley and began attending Avra Valley Community Church. Ron Reid became one of the Elders at that Church. God did what he wanted with that family.

From that point on Bert has been called to preach at Avra Valley Community Church many times. That entire family followed on with Jesus until, first Kenneth Chambers went home to be with the Lord and then a few years later Ruth also went home to be with Jesus as did their daughter Cheryl, Ron Reid's wife.

Chapter SEVENTEEN
Hope Alliance Church
An Inner-City Ministry, Oh, Really Lord

God leads us again.

"I'm just going to visit with Fred Allan today, the Pastor of Hope Alliance Church."

"Are you really sure?"

"I just need to do that, see if he needs some encouragement. We're not going there but I have to visit with him."

"Sure, you are."

God is just so patient. He knew we wanted to completely follow Him. That had always been our desire and he also knew we needed His renewal.

Here we go again. God was calling us, this time, to Hope Alliance Church, we couldn't get away from that. In Bert's words to me "over and over, I wouldn't go to Hope if it was the last

Alliance Church in the world." You'd think we could have learned by now not to say, "no, not that place."

"Bert, I'm giving you the keys and the books of the Church." Fred knew that he and his wife were being called away. In the near future, God did call Rev. Fred and Sonja Allan as missionaries to Europe some time later.

God was leading but the South Pacific District said all funds would be discontinued for Hope Alliance Church. Up to this point, the Allan's lived from District Subsidy for 2 years. We would have no district money to run the church. What was a mission church to do? Its people were on Medicaid and the ones that came in directly off the streets had already spent their welfare check on Alcohol and drugs for the most part. Life isn't easy for families on welfare. They came to a storefront church that had been founded by Rev. Joel Comiskey, Missionary to Ecuador, South America and in the Cell group movement.

Bert asked permission to do deputation work in the District (Oh, yeah. I remember. Someone said, "I don't want to do deputation work"). However, this would be the only way to bring in support from Alliance Churches in the South Pacific District. This had never been done before, but Bert inquired of Rev. Thompson, interim District Superintendent.

As it was the church had approximately $255.00 in the bank for operating expenses. Not even enough to pay the Month's rent of $735 per month. How would we survive? There were people who were workers in the church, but Bert gave everyone the option to leave or stay. 33 people from the congregation left.

"God, what are we doing? What is your plan?"

It was also here that God gave us the plan to start a newsletter that would go to every church not only in the District but also to every Church we had served in. The newsletter had to meet certain criteria. It had to be mailed at precisely the correct time of the month but it would never ask for support but rather it presented the needs of the church and asked for prayer. It couldn't be just one-sided, we had to commit to pray for our supporters as well.

It also had to include testimonies of the people who had come to know Jesus through the ministry at Hope Alliance Church. We did this for the 15 ½ years we ministered at Hope Alliance Church and sent out that letter every month. The funds did come in, not much from the congregation but from people of God. When and where God calls, we will follow, no matter what our opinion has been in the past. I think I remember. God is so good and just so patient with his people.

The storefront building the Church was worshiping in happened to be a historical building owned by the District Attorney of Long Beach California. She called Bert one day to ask if we were interested in enlarging the area we were using.

"I wanted to offer this to you first. Otherwise, if you don't take it, I have to rent it out to someone else. That might not be conducive to your Church."

"I don't know how we can afford it. We are barely bringing in enough to pay the rent on what we have already." Bert was serious.

"I'll give it to you at a lesser amount." She offered the amount, and we went to prayer.

We had been invited to speak at one of the California Alliance churches so we asked the people of Hope Alliance Church if some of our people from Hope Alliance Church would like to come with us and share their testimony, as Bert would present the needs of our Inner-City Ministry.

One of our people, a retired Honda Car Dealership Owner, was one of our guests. As it happened, he had to carry a *bag* due to illnesses he had been through.

Bert presented our needs and shared the testimonies.

All went well, and then one of the members of that Church came and said, "What is that smell? Don't your people ever bathe?"

Understand, these were people of God who couldn't fathom the problem we face frequently. Unknown to us, our retired Honda Dealership owner had a slight accident and he experienced a leak in his bag. One of our people quickly drove him home so that he could deal with his problem.

We had fellowship with the Church after our presentation. When we arrived home, Bert had a call from that Pastor of the Church.

"Pastor Bert, someone in our congregation has offered to pay the rent for the extension to your space for a 3-year period."

I'm very sure we had a jaw-dropping incident when we heard the news. God has a sense of humor and uses people when we least expect it in whatever capacity.

On one of our Vacations, as our habit has always been, to visit some of our previous ministries. We did that and decided to return to Joyce Bible Church and of course, Bert was asked to preach. He presented the needs of our church and could they please pray.

As we fellowshipped with them after the service, it was suggested, "Why don't we send our youth up to your church. Surely that would be a ministry for them."

From there the plan was concocted. The youth of Joyce Bible Church had decided they would like to visit our church in Long Beach and assist in any way possible. Their ministry with us would be over a 2-week period. We had the people in the Church provide them with a meal in their home and offer each of the youth showers. The youth stayed in the Church overnight. Then we would teach them the *Street-smarts*, or the *do's and don'ts* of street ministry.

It became such an awesome success that every year from that time on we invited youth from different Alliance Churches to come help us. We called it a *Youth Takeover*.

We also started a Church fellowship of Churches from our surrounding area every year to a time of singing and sharing talents from each church ending in a pot luck dinner. It also was a resounding success. We did these fellowships four times a year.

That year was a full year in every way imaginable. We had a call from My husband's brother, Jim. It would be important that we should come up because my mother-in-law was not likely to survive the night. We quickly packed the car and drove up through the snow. It was like a white-out by the time we made it to Bellingham, Washington. We chose to lay over in the rest stop until the snow would let up to enable us to drive up more safely.

We drove into Vancouver and were then notified that she had already passed away that night before. We stayed for the funeral and then had to drive back.

That same year the day came for the Long Beach Riots. They began in full force in the Los Angeles area and spread rapidly into our area in Long Beach. That included our location for Hope Alliance Church. We were in prayer for the upstairs renters of the building our Church was in. The neighbors patrolled the Church while one of the lady renters stood on guard on the rooftop. Buildings around us were being destroyed but Hope Alliance Church stood unscathed.

However, as this was happening, I had a phone call from my brother to say that my Mother had just been taken to the hospital with a stroke. We were torn between going to be with my Mother in Vancouver, or would Bert stay. He was also a Police Chaplain for the Long Beach Police Department. Should he stay or go with me. I knew I had to go.

We did go but we had to skirt the city to get past the rioting. We took the far north part of the Freeway to bypass the fighting. Even as we proceeded north, rioters threw bricks at our car but by the grace of God, they were unable to reach our car.

My mother was then in the hospital for six months before she passed away. She had been waiting for God to call her home, and now was the time. Of course, that meant another long haul to Vancouver, B.C. but I was able to see her at peace with her Savior.

We ministered At Hope Alliance Church for 15 ½ years and to God be the glory for the people whom God called. We had a worship team that had come off of drugs and alcohol and ministering like only they could.

Now, currently, Rev. Brian Smith, one such man God called from the streets is the Pastor. Employed with Boeing, he has become Ordained with The Alliance and carries the work forward. Praise God from whom all blessings flow.

During these days I worked, not necessarily because I wanted but to subsidize this ministry. At one point in our ministry at the Church, one of the ladies in the church said to me, "We feel you should be here for us during the day. You shouldn't have an outside job to keep you away from ministering to us."

I said, "I'm so sorry to hear you say that." We couldn't even afford to live in Long Beach because of the expense so instead we were able to buy a Condo in Garden Grove, California, 17 miles east of Long Beach.

I worked in Long Beach, just a few miles from the church. Of course, I loved the work as a loan specialist. Doesn't sound like the job for a Pastor's wife? But it worked for us.

Working alongside Bert as he pastored this Church, I began seriously working on my writing career. I had already delved into it earlier but now I began in earnestness. With all the busyness of ministry and work, it was a slow process but my passion for writing wouldn't quit. I plowed through my classes I had been taking. Planning toward retirement would be the beginning of my dream. I was able to retire from LBS Financial Credit Union also after 15 ½ years. Finally, I would have some kind of retirement. I'm saying I retired because Bert in theory had retired but then didn't.

Chapter EIGHTEEN
CrossPoint Community Church

With retirement approaching for me and knowing God was once again calling, we began to check out the land to see where God would lead. First, we checked out the *California Pines* further up in Northern California. We saw the ads on TV and thought, this might just be the place to retire. We checked out the location, unannounced and quickly discovered that people were being wined and dined, which included, and in fine print, the purchase of a lot with a Mobile Home. I inquired about the so-called lake as advertised.

"It's being dammed upstream."

Okay, so no lake. That answered all our questions.

We quickly discovered when people woke up from their property purchase, they immediately listed it for sale. So much for that land search. Being, we were still 5 years out from retiring, desperation was not in view.

Another area we could cross off our list. We checked out Escondido and visited with the Pastor of the Alliance Church. It could have been a place of ministry though we knew we were not called to that area. We really didn't have any desire to go as far as Tucson, Arizona, because that would take us away from the coast and we had spent most of our lives up and down the coast. Would God call us away from that?

We finally did check out Tucson, thinking it would be better than the busyness of Phoenix, though Flagstaff gave me some pull. Then we told the Lord, our needs.

"Lord, if you want us in Tucson, we need a Church to serve in."

"But, Lord, not only that, we need a Costco to shop at."

We didn't stop there. "The town must also have a Starbucks for us to work in." Not that we couldn't work at home. What do you think? Would God answer such a selfish prayer?

Of course, we needed to buy a house, sell our home in Garden Grove. What do you think?

The economy had just stepped up a bit, so why not, would God be pleased with our request?

We had already searched Casa Grande where they had multiple new builds. Large homes for not a lot of money but the Alliance Church had just closed. The hospital would do, knowing we would be traveling to Phoenix for most of our needs.

Now, I had a special request for the buying of our home. I needed what I call a square grid because I need to be able to find my way. We could have done that the easy way and used a realtor but why? We searched for homes and places, and then new builds. We tried Sahuarita, Arizona near Green Valley but they had no smaller homes for display. We drove from there to where we actually live now and saw what we might want.

Still, we needed to check out the Church. CrossPoint Community, would they want our services? Would we fit in with these desert people? Surely enough Rev. Jim Corley was already a very good friend of ours from the Pacific Northwest District. The Church said yes. Then we found there was not just one Costco but two Costco's in town. We proceed to the local Starbucks. It wasn't large but it was there.

We drove home and prayed a lot. God had given us a yes at every corner, everything to make life pleasant for us, was available. Was this where He wanted us? I had pertinent requests such as the house we were buying had to have a tile roof. We didn't want a large house because that wouldn't be prudent for us over the long term. Checking it out we found many reasonable houses but not my grid.

Finally, there it was. The tile roof, open concept, and of course, the price was right. It also had my grid. Now God had given us a Church very close to our resident, a Starbucks just up the road from us and two Costco's. It was more than I imagined. A Pet Veterinarian on the street just near us (for our dog) as well as a Credit Union on the same street. All more than I could've hoped for.

God always requires obedience first. We put our house on the market, drove back to Tucson and put our down payment on the house so that the builders could start to build our house.

Our realtor had us stage our Condo in Garden Grove, California for sale which meant we had to put most of our belongings into storage.

Fortunately for us, our good friend, John Zimmermann offered to let us store all our belongings in his garage until we would be able to sort everything out or until our move to Arizona. John and Beth Zimmermann had worked with us in the founding of Fountain of Life Church, in Fountain Valley, California and they are the parents of Robbie Zimmerman, who Bert had mentored for his Ordination just months earlier in The Alliance.

Our house then sold within a day of listing. This meant we would have to move out within the 60 days of closing but the house we were buying wasn't yet finished. We had wanted to buy a motor home anyhow so that would enable us to escape the hot summers in Tucson if we wished. As a result, we lived in our motorhome for 6 months in Anaheim, California, a mile from Disneyland while we finished up our Long Beach ministries.

I retired from Long Beach Schools Credit Union and Bert resigned from the ministries of Hope Alliance Church. I still have communication with the people at the Credit Union and of course, we also stay in touch with the Pastor of HAC, Brian Smith whom Bert also mentored being that Bert serves on Licensing, Ordination and Consecration Council of The Alliance.

Finally, we were able to plan our move to Tucson Arizona. It appeared that I would have to drive the car following Bert into Arizona. I was not liking that. We have a wonderful friend in Phoenix whom we conscripted or asked if he would help and drive the U-Haul for us as Bert drove the car. We were driving down Interstate 10 and at each stop, Bert would ask Joe Ely if we should stop for gas.

"We need to gas up, Joe?"

"No, I don't think so Bert, the gauge still says the gas tank is almost full. We should be fine."

We were driving toward Casa Grande when suddenly Joe pulled the U-Haul over, tipping halfway into the ravine.

"Bert, the U-Haul is going to tip. There goes our life, everything we own is in it!"

Marie (Joe's wife who was riding with us in our car) said, "But there goes my husband."

You guessed it. He ran out of gas because he was looking at the wrong gauge. We called the Auto Club and shortly thereafter, they arrived and to give us a gallon of gas so that we could proceed to the next gas station.

We got moved and all our belongs were put into the garage of our new home for when we would finally leave Hope Alliance Church.

We arrived at CrossPoint, hitting the ground running. Rev. Jim Corley was into Cell groups and home ministries. We were immediately asked to have an open house and invite the neighborhood and the churches over to our house.

I'm glad I was still young at the time. I still had the energy to comply and we did enjoy it. Our neighbors came to know us and some of them came to know Jesus.

This was interrupted temporarily as Alliance Bible Church called Bert to become the Interim pastor for a one-year period.

Rev. Kelvin Benton and his family came later and resumed the ministry at Alliance Bible Church. We went back to CrossPoint Community Church where Bert became one of the Associate Pastors.

One memorable event we had was our 10-year anniversary celebration with a Pig Feast at CrossPoint Community Church. The preparation for that in itself was a part of the celebration with the digging of the pit, burying an entire pig and roasting it on the embers. Then came the festival of celebration.

CrossPoint under Jim Corley's ministry had several Pastors that were active in the Church and shared in the Preaching of the Word. The church also had the Noah's Day Care that was a very successful and important entity of the Church.

Then one day a family from Green Valley called Pastor Jim Corley and pleaded with him to start a church in their area. It wasn't long before we were asked if we would do a Church Plant in Green Valley. Thus, we were assigned the job of planting a Church in Green Valley with some success.

CrossPoint Community Church had an extensive Cell ministry under the leadership of Dr. Joel Comiskey, the same pastor that founded Hope Alliance Church, in Long Beach, California.

During our time at CrossPoint, we were given the task to obtain a license for Kid Arizona, a ministry to troubled families and their children. The late Gilbert Cardoza was the founding Counselor that gave special classes as required and assigned by the Courts to give classes on stress management as well as family relations. We also went into the local schools in Tucson to teach the teens before leaving the school system not to follow the drug and alcohol scene. Gilbert gave them all the reasons and had a special rapport with the teens and was very well accepted. That was Kid Arizona, Bert headed up until Gilbert Carrizosa passed away.

Then one day, we were given the news that as Tucson is a Military Town, and David Monthan Airforce flight pattern had been changed to fly over the church, there now was a problem. The city decided they could not risk the lives of children should a flight mishap happen over the church while the daycare was in session. As a result, though Pastor Jim had previously had clearance to purchase the 10 acres of land to build the church, they wanted it closed and they would buy it.

We watched as other churches came into the neighborhood without any problems, however, we had a very active day care center which was an important part of the church and likely the reason.

It resulted in all the Pastors of CrossPoint resigning and moving on to other ministries. That meant us as well. However, we remained in Tucson, thinking, "What now Lord?"

My Journey on the Road to Emmaus   Diana E. Linn

Chapter **NINETEEN**
Alliance Bible Church, Tucson, Arizona

After the closure of CrossPoint Community Church, we returned to Alliance Bible Church with Rev. Calvin Benton as pastor.

Then in 2010, after coming back from a Vacation in the Yukon and after returning from Truth or Consequence Alliance Church, in New Mexico, for the Pastor's Ordination Installation Service, my dear husband, Bert took ill. He spent a month in the hospital in an induced coma which the doctors did to aid in his healing.

Every day I spent 8 hours siting with Bert so that I could be there and speak to the Doctors as they came in to care for him. Every day I wrote emails to everyone to report the progress as God gave me scriptures for his situation. God also gave me the assurance that he would come through this and once again be active in the ministry.

People would come to visit him and some would say, "I'll be back when he is no longer in the coma." I knew perfectly well some didn't believe God could bring him through. But then again, I had that assurance from God and who was I to question God.

Then there were people that stood by me as I waited on God. Dr. Alan Rosenburg, one of Bert's colleagues from LOCC, would pray with me every evening for Bert's healing.

When the medical profession was about to give up on Bert's healing, God sent, I believe, a Doctor ordained of God who had the wisdom and a plan that would heal Bert's illnesses. God healed and again answered prayer, though now he had to learn to walk, work and preach again. By the grace of God, He did and we continue to serve in the ministry as God continues to call.

On August 1 of 2010, a call was given to Rev. Mike Farlin and Cornise to Pastor Alliance Bible Church. Under Pastor Mike's ministry, Bert became the Associate Pastor with Rev. Farlin at Alliance Bible Church in Tucson from 2010 until 2018.

This is the Church where God used Bert to impart the Great Commission Ministry Series, teaching the basics of who God is, the deeper life sessions. Bert preached and taught how to equip God's people as they live in our world, a dying world who without Christ will die in their sins.

Bert led Boot Camps in learning to share in Lifestyle Evangelism as well in the Coffee Shop ministry locally in Tucson. Witnessing to the people around us and inviting them to Jesus, our Savior. At the end of one session, we photographed a group picture that was presented to students for their graduation.

My husband has also had the privilege of mentoring a few of the Pastors in town for which we praise God. Bert continues to preach and to teach seminars on being a Great Commission Christian. The How-To's of our living faith.

On two separate occasions, Bert has had the privilege to officiate in the renewing of Wedding Vows for two separate couples. One such couple from Saskatchewan, after 50 years of marriage and more recently a couple, for their 50th Anniversary renewing vows who were from the Wesleyan Church serving in Dragoon Baptist Church in Dragoon, Arizona.

Life doesn't stop there for either my husband or I. At the same time, he preaches at different churches around the Tucson and outlying areas. Bert has also been preaching at Avra Valley Community Church just 40 miles west of Tucson. We thank God, that he has opened doors for ministry around the area. Between Bert's mentoring, serving on the Licensing, Ordination, Consecration Council, of the South Pacific Alliance, and preaching whenever he can, we enjoy being involved in ministry in mentoring to young men and women preparing for Alliance Ministry.

My Journey on the Road to Emmaus   Diana E. Linn

Chapter **TWENTY**
The Road Church, Tucson, Arizona

We haven't stopped or retired yet. As the writing of my memoirs, My Journey on the Road to Emmaus, we now worship with The Road Church under the Pastoral Leadership of Rev. Sam Wright (whom Bert also mentored through his Ordination into The Alliance). Now Rev. Sam Wright is my husband's boss, at least in the local church.

God has also given my husband many Preaching Engagements in churches and in our later years. *"Do not cast me off in the time of old age; forsake me not when my strength is spent"* (Psalm 71:9). That is our prayer for the ministry God is still giving us.

My Journey on the Road to Emmaus   Diana E. Linn

Chapter **TWENTY-ONE**
Epilogue
"But, the End is Not Yet" (Mark 13:7)

    What's our future ministry together? We are still busy, Bert is involved with Licensing, Ordination and Consecration with the South Pacific Alliance. His mentoring with men and women that have been called into the ministry is still a part of his life.

    To this date, I have written four Novels. ***Can Anyone Tell Me? ... The Romanov Dynasty ... What If? ... Abducted and Lost ...*** and ***Life Runs Uneven***. These are all fiction based on fact and now, ***My Emmaus Road Journey, Memoirs of a Pastor's Wife***, is entirely based on true ministry reality. The personal truth is that God impressed upon my heart that now was the time to write my memoirs. Therefore, I did. These books are all available on Amazon.com and BarnesandNobles.com. ***My Emmaus Road Journey, Memoirs of a Pastor's Wife***, is coming soon.

    Bert wrote, ***Memoirs of an Inner City Pastor, Righteously Walking on the Side of Danger,*** a few years earlier and he stated, this is "my jab" at our Alliance Memoirs of a Pastor's Life together. Headquarters in Colorado asked for a copy of this. So, it's sitting on the third shelf from the bottom of a Bookcase collecting dust, dirt and memories on how not to pastor in *The Alliance*.

I also write a Newsletter that I publish every other month and it is in there that I write articles that apply to what is currently happening in our society and of course, those are non-fiction.

Why do I write fiction? It allows me to permeate the untouched areas of life. Situations we prefer to rub out of our memories, mostly because we haven't yet come to the place of complete surrender to Jesus. However, God has a way. He has a beautiful plan for all of us even when the world has totally turned on us.

We are so precious in God's sight that Jesus died for us. We might think our sins are so horrible that there is no chance of a normal life. That is just not true. All we have to do is confess our sins, ask Him to forgive us and God promises to do that.

We often blame ourselves for what we do, but we can ask God for forgiveness, and guess what, God takes it away. It is now under the blood, never to be remembered again, as far as the *east is from the west*. Then, of course, we have to turn around and not repeat what we have done. You say, "How can I do that?"

God in your weakness will guide you, pull you to himself. He will walk with you even when you are being tempted. God does not want us to suffer through unimaginable situations alone. He wants to be there with you. You will come out at the other end victorious, simply trust Him.

For now, I will leave the Non-Fiction writing up to my dear husband, the Pastor for the people, for the lost as he leads them to Jesus. Hold on there, isn't that exactly what my books are all about? Indeed, they are. Every one of them is intended to share the message that God has for me to share with people. My novels are intended to probe into the instances nobody talks about and how those instances shape our lives. Then how God can intervene and remedy those situations.

It isn't so much, if you follow this plan, you'll never have to face the unreasonable. Let me tell you, you will be facing the unreasonable even when you do nothing but make the right choices for your life. You say, "Is that statement true?" I say it is and that's why I feel God has given me just a slice of what He wants me to share.

You say, "That can't be. You're talking Murder Mysteries."

Aren't those the hard times' none of us want to walk through? It is this that God gives me and I want to use for His Glory.

My choice of genre is fiction, finding it opens opportunities to punch through those dark corners of our lives that we often find we have to live through. God has given me real incidences that have a story to show, not just tell. We can only get through difficult circumstances that are too horrific to endure but with the grace of God's help. So, I write about it.

There is always a way, God makes that way of escape but we must follow. Our answers are not always just on the page, or "thus saith the Lord." Indeed, His word is always the final authority but sometimes we have to walk through very narrow passages that are hard to find but for the Grace of God. "He does make the way straight" so that we can obediently follow.

My husband is still preparing Seminars, preaching and teaching. We wait on God for leading and leading will come as we are co-workers together. So, if you are interested, contact us at e-mail: bertlinn03@icloud.com

I had a dream that was being formulated over the years. I had a desire to write for most of my adult years. I allowed God to lead me in my learning pursuits to deepen my compassion for writing.

When the Christian Writer's Guild existed, the owner was Jerry Jenkins who is the co-author of the best seller, "The Left Behind Series." I enrolled in two extensive classes with them and now I have become my own publisher. I am still in the learning process of the publishing business and my Web Page but have had some success. My training for writing started in the '80s but my passion for writing started in grade school. The desire to tell the story with a Christian message has not yet been taken from me.

This is definitely not the end. If anything, it is the beginning of new challenges that we desire to share. God has thus far given us the years, but those years do belong to Him. It is for me and for Bert the desire of our hearts to serve Him all the days of our lives.

Sometimes it seems the whole world is coming apart. Then I say, Jesus is coming soon, *"When these things begin to take place, stand up and lift up your heads because your redemption is drawing near"* (Luke 21:28).

Even so, Onward, Upward, Forward, we continue on with The Road Church, a Church of the Christian and Missionary Alliance. Pressing forward, we continue to serve as God leads.

THE END

ONE LAST THING

I hope you enjoyed reading **"My Journey on the Road to Emmaus, Memoirs of a Pastor's Wife."** My husband and I want to see you in eternity. However, if you have not made your *"Peace with God"* as yet, I trust you will read on and accept the Lord as your personal Savior.

Romans 3:23
"for all have sinned and fall short of the glory of God"
Romans 6:23
"For the wages of sin is death, but the gift of God is eternal life through Christ Jesus our Lord."
John 1:12
'Yet to all who did receive him, to those who believed in his name, he gave the right to become children of God"
Romans 10:9-10
 "If you declare with your mouth, "Jesus is Lord," and believe in your heart that God raised him from the dead, you will be saved. For it is with your heart that you believe and are justified, and it is with your mouth that you profess your faith and are saved."
John 3:18 NKJV
 "He who believes in Him is not condemned; but he who does not believe is condemned already,   because he has not believed in the name of the only begotten Son of God."

.

**Printed in
Tucson Arizona
2019**

My Journey on the Road to Emmaus   Diana E. Linn

**A Short Testimony of
Bert & Diana Linn**

Bert's Testimony

Early childhood, generally speaking, was happy and content. The domestic background was lovingly seasoned with good old-fashioned Scottish upbringing discipline and heritage. We lacked for nothing. According to my parents, if asked their spiritual background, without any hesitancy, loud and clear—"United Church of Canada—and if everyone was as good and honest and hard working as we are this would be a better world to live in." Thus, was my childhood as I grew up in Canada and the beautiful city of Vancouver, British Colombia.

Upon high school graduation in June of 1957, it was time to think of the future and the "mark you are to put on this world." I was told, "Your grandfather and his father took to the sea. Your father left university and a student of dentistry to fight for his country." After the war he entered the construction field. I, as a result chose to become an apprentice electrician and four years later a journeyman Aircraft Electrician. Now ... A Journeyman Electrician, making good money ... young and healthy, everything ahead, and nothing behind. Why was I not happy—I was soon to find out I needed Christ.

I came to know Christ at Capitol Hill Alliance Church in Vancouver B.C. while listening to a Moody Bible Institute Evangelist Preach ... From there it was a ministry hop ... skip ... and a jump.

My Journey on the Road to Emmaus — Diana E. Linn

Diana's Testimony

I was born to an American father and a Russian mother at the end of the great depression. By the time I was four years old we moved from Winnipeg to Vancouver, B.C. but when I was nine, we moved to Burnaby and that's where God spoke to me to come to Him. I recall the strong conviction of the Holy Spirit as I knelt at my chair in the Salvation Army Sunday School. It was here I asked the Lord to save me. It wasn't long before I attended Capitol Hill Alliance. Soaking up the biblical truth from Pastor and Mrs. Hauge's biblical teaching.

After College, I came back to my home Church where I met my husband who was now between pastorates and living with his parents. February, 1972, we married and accepted a call to ministry in Joyce, Washington. From there we have served in Washington … Oregon … California and now Tucson, Arizona.

Currently Bert and I worship at The Road Church, a Church of The Alliance in Tucson, Arizona.

My Journey on the Road to EmmausDiana E. Linn

BIOGRAPHICAL HISTORY – FOR DIANA E. LINN

Diana E. Linn was born 1938 in Winnipeg, Manitoba, Canada. Her family moved to Vancouver, British Columbia, 1942.
She received her early education in Burnaby, British Columbia. Diana earned an Associate of Arts Degree from Fresno Pacific University in Fresno, California in 1963.
Diana and Bert married in 1972 at Capitol Hill Alliance Church in North Burnaby, British Columbia, Canada. Diana's Hobbies are: Photography, Photography Restoration, Oil Painting, Model Building.

Diana's Education Bio

1962 – 1963   Associate of Arts Degree, Fresno Pacific College (University), Fresno, California

1980 –   Graduated School of Modern Photography, Little Falls, New Jersey

1982 –   Veronica Cass National School of Retouching, Inc., Seattle, Washington

1994 –   The Laural School of Bookkeeping and Accounting, Phoenix, Arizona

1997 –   ICS Learning Systems, Inc., Scranton, Pennsylvania, on Short Story Writing/Journalism

1998 –   ICS Learning Systems, Inc., Scranton, Pennsylvania, on Master Art

2003 – 2006   Completed Studies with Jerry Jenkins, Christian Writer's Guild, Black Forest, CO

Diana's working career outside of the ministry:

1957 – 1962   Pumps & Power, Pump manufacturing business, as Cost Accounting Clerk, Vancouver, British Columbia, Canada

1962 – 1963   Fresno Lutheran Church, Church Secretary, Fresno, California

1963, – 1969   Canadian Kenworth, Truck Manufacturing Co., Cost Accounting, Vancouver, British Columbia, Canada

1969 – 1972   Galbraith & Sully/Robert Morse, Cost Accounting, Vancouver, British Columbia, Canada

1976 – 1980   Capitol Savings and Loan, Mortgage Lending, Olympia, Washington

1984 – 1988   Umpqua Federal Credit Union/Roseburg Federal Credit Union, Teller, Loan Specialist, Roseburg, Oregon

1988 – 2003   LBS Financial Credit Union, Loan Specialist, Long Beach, California

Churches Served as a Pastor's Wife

1971 – 1975   Joyce Bible Church, Joyce, Washington
Teaching emphasis on Life Style Evangelism

1975 – 1980   Shelton Alliance Church, Shelton, Washington
Emphasis on Evangelism Outreach

1980 – 1984   Roseburg Alliance Church, Roseburg, Oregon
Emphasis on Marriage Counselling

1984 – 1988   Long Beach Rescue Mission, Long Beach, California
House Mother at Lydia House-Weekly Bible Teaching with the women

1988 – 1991   Fountain of Life Church, Fountain Valley, California
Emphasis on Outreach, Evangelism and Discipleship Training

1991-2003   Hope Alliance Church, Long Beach, California
Inner-City Mission Church

2003-2006   CrossPoint Community Church, Tucson Arizona
Emphasis on Cell Group Ministries

2006-2018   Alliance Bible Church, Tucson, Arizona
Emphasis on Teaching Life Style Discipleship Seminars

2003-to present
Books Authored:

- *Can Anyone Tell Me?*
- *The Romanov Dynasty … What If?*
- *Abducted and Lost*
- *Life Runs Uneven*
- *Memoirs of a Pastor's Wife* **(newest book, 2019)**

END NOTES

Ministry Photographs were taken by B & D Photography (Bert & Diana Linn).
Historical photographs are used by permission and/or are in Public Domain.

www.ingramcontent.com/pod-product-compliance
Lightning Source LLC
Chambersburg PA
CBHW070559010526
44118CB00012B/1377